W9-COP-660

DISCARDED

Jeanne Tsatsos

Ιōanna Tsatsou

The Sword's Fierce Edge

A Journal
of the
Occupation of Greece,
1941–1944

ἀπὸ τὴν κόψη τοῦ σπαθιοῦ τὴν τρομερή.

Authorized English Translation
by Jean Demos

Vanderbilt University Press
1969

Standard Book Number 8265–1139–2
Library of Congress Catalogue
Card number 76–89473

Printed in the United States of America
by Heritage Printers, Inc.
Charlotte, North Carolina

Contents

Historical Note   v

Foreword   xi

1941   1

1942   19

1943   39

1944   91

Index   127

Historical Note

AT DAWN on October 28, 1940, without any warning, Mussolini invaded Greek soil from Italian-occupied Albania.

At first the Greeks defended themselves, then passed from defense to attack, entered Albanian territory, which was then also Italian territory, and seized the two most important cities of Southern Albania, Koritsa and Argyrocastro. This was the first Allied victory of the Second World War.

From December 1940 to April 1941 the Italians tried in vain to drive out the Greeks. The Greek troops were entrenched in enemy soil. Germany reasoned that these first defeats of the Axis dangerously diminished the prestige of Mussolini and thus affected the whole development of the war. Indeed, they created a situation which began to influence the entire strategy of the German General Staff. For these reasons Hitler decided to invade Greece from the Jugoslavian and Bulgarian borders with his mechanized forces and to attack the Greek army from the south where it was deployed against the Italian army within Albanian territory. This attack took place on April 6, 1941. Thus little Greece with eight million inhabitants was obliged to confront Italy with its forty million and Germany with its sixty million. At that point the British sent to Greece's aid airplanes and land forces from the Middle East.

The Greek resistance could not possibly hold out against this double attack. One part of the Greek army disintegrated; another part with newly arrived British troops—most of them New Zealanders and Australians—covered the retreat, with the aim of

v

enabling as many of their forces as possible to reach Crete, where they would continue the resistance. The German Stoukas continuously bombed the Greek ports and the Greek ships, both war and merchant ships, which were leaving for Crete. A few days later the most select units of German parachutists began the offensive against Crete. More than twelve thousand parachutists were killed in this attack. Today we know that if the Middle East Command had continued the resistance in Crete for another twenty-four hours the Germans would have given up the struggle. The size of their losses was disproportionate to the advantage to be derived from occupying the island.

Earlier, King George II, the Greek Government, a part of the administrative staff, and small units of the armed forces had been concentrated on Crete, but now the Greek struggle was transferred to the Middle East. The King, Crown Prince Paul, and the royal family were established in Cairo, along with the government of Free Greece and what remained of the apparatus of the state. There they began to organize armed land forces from all those who had fled Greece and from the Greeks of Egypt and Cyprus whose number exceeded a half million. Alexandria became the principal base of the Greek navy.

In Greece, already occupied by the Germans and Italians, among ruins caused by the bombings—Athens was not bombed—wandered thousands of British troops who had not been able to escape. All these now tried by every possible means to get away to the Middle East so as to continue the fight. At the same time, an enormous problem of food supply was building up because the conquerors took all the food.

From the very beginning, almost without exception, the Greek people instinctively concealed the British who were scattered throughout Southern Greece, fed them in spite of the famine, and helped them to escape arrest. But naturally sending them to Egypt required some organization. In a few weeks, in collaboration with the Middle East Command, many groups were created to organize the sending of great numbers of men to Egypt, Syria, and Palestine.

Of necessity, this was the first form of resistance. But the whole body of the Greek people asked to be organized to fight the enemy in various ways. Thus, at the end of 1941, the universal Greek resistance began to take shape.

Mainly in the mountainous regions of the country, from Olympus and the Pindus range as far as Taygetos, it was usually led by Greek army officers, to whom planes from the Middle East Army dropped weapons. From the beginning, radio contact between these groups and the Middle East was good, and it continued to improve with time.

Even in the cities, resistance groups were organized; their members were chiefly officers with radio equipment at their disposal, and their purpose was to transmit information to the Middle East Command. These groups also undertook sabotage operations in the ports and supply centers. Three main resistance groups eventually emerged: the EDES of Zervas, the EKKA of Psarros, and the EAM-ELAS which, without anyone suspecting it, took its orders from the Communist party.

The Church, with Archbishop Damaskinos at its head, played a major role as always in Greek history, supporting the resistance and helping the people to survive.

This is the historic frame in which *The Sword's Fierce Edge* is set.

Time brings the truth to light.

Menander

Foreword

I DID not intend this journal for publication. I wrote, and from time to time I dropped my pages into a tin box buried in a corner of our garden, so that sometime our children might read them.

More than twenty years have passed, and I see that the events which shook the nation have been forgotten. The psychological climate of that epoch has entirely disappeared.

And yet thousands of Greek women had felt as I felt and acted as I acted. My own life, as I had lived it, was almost the universal experience of the Greek woman. I believe it is a duty to preserve this in our memory.

Moreover, the position in which I chanced to be at that time gave me the opportunity to know the spirit and the deeds of some exceptional men and women, superb in their heroism. I considered it my obligation to commemorate all that I had witnessed of their lives so that they should stand as lessons and examples in times when national ideals may not hold the dominant place which they then had.

I hope I shall be forgiven many omissions and imperfections of various kinds.

I present unaltered a text which is a piece of my life. As I cannot change my life which is passed, so I could not change these pages, nor did I wish to change them.

J.T.

1941

Thou hast enlarged me when I was in distress.

Psalms 4:1

14 September 1941

I sit on the small veranda near the dining room, hoping to cool off a little.[1] Slowly, slowly the soft September light dissolves into night. There is a knock at the door and Katina Doussi enters. Katina is a neighbor, poor, but very clever. Now she speaks quickly; she is frightened and desperate.

"My lady, a blond archangel just came to my house. I locked him in the kitchen. What is to become of him? The man who brought him disappeared."

"An officer?" I asked.

"I think so."

"All right. Go back home. Close your door securely, and don't let anyone in—not even your own people. I'll come right away."

This episode doesn't surprise me. Every so often we hear of some ally in danger or need. The working people help with all their hearts, but they have no way of aiding these men to escape, nor of feeding them. So we make up a chain of friends ready to support them.

I telephone immediately to George Averof, one of these friends. He brings me the key to an empty house, which he happens to have just now.

Into a bag I put some bread, canned goods, sugar, coffee, soap, and I go to Katina's house in Soteros Street.

Inside her little kitchen, reeking of fried fish, stands the Englishman, erect in a corner. His head almost touches the ceiling. He looks like a hunted bird. We exchange a few words and then go warily out into the street. I put my arm through his, and we walk along unconcerned.

George Averof and my husband follow at a distance.

We go toward Vouliagmeni Street. Every time we meet German patrols, I chatter Greek to him playfully. We turn into a side street. In my hand I have the key to the old house. We have no trouble finding it. The neighborhood is deserted. Inside everything is in order. We sit down comfortably and start to talk. He

[1] Our house, 9 Kydathineon Street, is located in that part of central Athens called Plaka.

3

has a great deal to tell me and he needs to talk. He is in love with a Greek girl and he does not want to leave Greece. He is willing to stay in hiding, to be in danger, if only he can see her. He talks and talks about his girl, and there is no end to it.

"And now, on top of everything else, we have to cope with lovers," I think to myself as I interrupt him. I tell him that it is late, that I will come again tomorrow to bring his food and to talk further with him. It is the only way I can get away.[2]

15 September 1941

I saw the Englishman at noon as we agreed. In the evening we moved him to another address.

I am glad about this. Every time I manage to help one of the British I have the added satisfaction of feeling that in some small degree we are combatting the violence of the conqueror. Because, whether by deceit or action, it is an absolute necessity for us somehow to oppose violence.

30 September 1941

The Italians have seized Lela Karayanni and her husband because they had hidden some Englishmen. But the two of them are confessing nothing. No secret escapes them.

Dangers lie in wait in most unlikely places. In order to protect our friends from ourselves, we try to know as little as possible. Just those things necessary for our work. But Lela Karyianni's activity was widespread. In her own caique she sent to Egypt whatever scattered Allies she could gather. Her name became known through indiscreet remarks.

---

[2] A little later, their marriage took place at the home of Admiral Alekos Levidis.

10 October 1941

Poor Levesque,[3] a profoundly intellectual man and a good friend, tried to escape at that frightful time when the Germans entered. But his ship was wrecked, and he came back in terrible shape. He is alone, helpless. How will he live, refined, cultivated man that he is, in these days when only the black marketeers can make a living?

We are thinking about organizing some classes in literature at our house, asking those who attend to pay something.

As a start this is a solution.

16 October 1941

Yesterday in the evening Levesque gave his first lecture. It was a great success. He took as his central theme *The Prodigal Son* by André Gide, and from there he went on to analyze ways in which other writers have worked over this parable from the Gospels. The drawing room, the dining room, the library were so full of people that we could hardly breathe. About eighty people sat—some on tables, some on Costakis' desk, feet folded under—and listened as if magnetized.

Instinctively we were returning to the old familiar intellectual atmosphere. The speaker's genuinely artistic spirit quieted the demons of hate and action that possess us since the beginning of our slavery.

18 October 1941

We spent the whole morning at Aghia Barbara.[4] Helpless Britons are scattered about there in the poor houses. Beside food and clothing, we took with us some sheets of paper with simple English words translated into Greek. All these foreign friends of ours must seem as little foreign as possible.

[3] Robert Levesque, a French writer and great Philhellene. He translated the poems of Sikelianos and Seferis.
[4] A suburb of Athens.

20 October 1941

Today we heard about the first irreparable disaster. At Eleusis some Greeks were executed. Yesterday the Germans shot three brave young men. A few days before, they confided their great grief to the priest who gave them communion: it was their concern for their wives and children, whom they were leaving without protection.

24 October 1941

The Archbishop Damaskinos has asked me to take on the families of those who were executed. I shall have help from his office. We will give them a monthly allowance, also clothing and food. I accepted this assignment gratefully.

27 October 1941

Today was a great day. As we opened the windows, the sun flooded the house. My husband[5] is supposed to have a lecture at the University tomorrow, the anniversary of the outbreak of the Greek-Italian War. But he informed his students that he would give it today instead, contrary to the order of the government,[6] because he considers the 28th of October to be a national holiday.

And so he gave the lecture today. Afterward, when he came home in the evening, he was accompanied by many young people. All of them had an expression of sadness but at the same time of pride. Moved by his words, they felt themselves "enslaved freemen."

Later, when we were alone, to pass the time, we decided to put the library in order. At that moment the bell of the outside door

[5] Constantine Tsatsos, professor of philosophy of law at the University of Athens.
[6] The Council of the University had also declared that the 28th of October would not be a holiday, and that consequently all classes would meet.

rings. I go myself to open it. A friend of ours from the Greek Security Police tells us that they are on their way to arrest my husband. We discuss for a moment what had better be done. We are undecided, but behind this persecution stands the enemy, and it is better that he leave home. So he takes off immediately and goes to the house of a good old friend.

Half an hour later, the doorbell rings again. I open the door. Three young men, one of whom reminds me of someone, ask for my husband. I say that he is not there. They want to know when he will come back. I say at nine o'clock that evening. They go away.

It is nearly eight. The children go to bed. Despina with her doll in her arms, Dora[7] with her Teddy, her big bear. Soon they are fast asleep. At nine the bell rings again. It is the same men.

"Mr. Tsatsos?"

"He isn't here."

They show their identity cards and say: "We are from the Greek Security Police. We are going to search the house." And they begin to search everywhere with their powerful flashlights. They look in the rooms, in the toilets, in the store rooms. They keep flashing their lights on Dora with her Teddy bear. They are puzzled by this great object lying there near the child. Fortunately Dora continues to sleep soundly.

After the search they tell me that they have been instructed to remain in the house, one inside and the other two watching the outer door.

And so the two go away, and the other stretches himself out in a deep armchair. Time passes. Eleven. Midnight. I am very sleepy.

The man who has remained in the house says to me: "I know Mr. Tsatsos. I arrested him under Metaxas."[8]

I look at him with pity.

"Aren't you too young to go on doing this work?" I ask him.

---

[7] My daughters Despina, age nine, and Dora, seven.

[8] C. Tsatsos was arrested and exiled in 1939, during the dictatorship, because he expressed himself against the regime.

He doesn't answer me. Perhaps he is ashamed, because after a little he says to me with some embarrassment:

"I must go down and see what the others are doing."

I close the door with relief and finally go to my bed.

28 October 1941

Such a triumphant national holiday I have never seen before. At seven o'clock the telephone began waking me, and from that moment it rang without stopping. The papers today write: "Constantine Tsatsos is dismissed and deprived of his pension." The house is full of people I know and others whom I do not. I have left the outer door open. Politicians, officers, and officials, common folk, all are here.

An unknown army captain asks to speak to me privately.

"Since the Albanian war, today for the first time I feel like a free man," he says to me softly. His eyes are misty with tears. "I want to give you something I happen to have," and shyly he brings out of his pocket a gold sovereign.

For a moment I am at a loss for words, moved by this man's feeling for us.

"I don't really need it now—if I should need it—" I whisper, fearing to offend him. "But thank you, truly I thank you."

Voices are heard in the street. I run to the balcony. The street is black with students. The young people, after placing flowers on the grave of the Unknown Soldier, are coming directly to our house.

"We—want—Tsa—tsos, we—want—Tsa—tsos," they shout in rhythm. "Tsatsos, another victim of the Axis."

The telephone rings persistently. I take the receiver. It is a police officer.

"Try to get the students to disperse," he says to me. "The Italians are coming!"

I run down the stairs, into the street, and say to the young people:

"The worst thing that could happen to your professor is that one of you should be hurt. I beg you to disperse, to go quietly to your homes. Soon we shall all be together again."

They understand, and slowly they begin to leave.[9]

Until late that night, the house is a shrine. The men from the Security Police continue to watch in the street below.

2 November 1941

The crowd has thinned out. Yesterday there was nobody. All day I was alone with my children and the Security Police who were guarding the street.

Today not even they. I went to the Plaka Distribution Center to give out milk. A work of hours because there were so many women. In the midst of the hubbub came Antigone, a fine girl from Plaka who had been my co-worker from the beginning of the war. She whispered in my ear.

"Go home. It is urgent."

I left my papers with another worker and hurried home. What should I see? The men of the Security Police had turned everything upside down. Our maid, Eudoxia, stood weeping and trembling in a corner of the dining room. My children were in their room, speechless. Their little faces lighted up when they saw me. I went back to the hall. The men had gathered around the telephone.

"What do you want?" I said to them. "Don't you understand that Tsatsos is in hiding? This is the third time you have searched us. Why do you bother us? Against whom are you waging this war of nerves? Against my little children when I am away? While we are distributing milk to people who are dying of hunger?"

One of them got up, took the receiver, and said loudly, in order to frighten me: "This is a job for the Italians."

"Maybe they are better than you are," I answered and turned my back on them.

[9] The Italians arrested seven of these young people, the most active ones. Three days later, after having beaten them in order to draw out charges against Tsatsos, they released them.

4 November 1941

Nobody appeared today, neither a good man nor a bad one. At the University the students continue to shout in rhythm: "We —want—Tsa—tsos, we—want—Tsa—tsos," stamping their feet and beating their desks.

5 November 1941

A frightful atmosphere. In every direction an impasse. I don't want to speak to anybody about ourselves. I am ashamed of slavery as I am ashamed of ugliness.

7 November 1941

This morning Archbishop Damaskinos telephoned. All these days he has been at Salamis at the monastery of Phaneromeni. As soon as he returned and was informed of what had happened at the University, he called me to his office. For the first time, I saw him at close hand and gave him an account of events. He listened attentively and then said to me, "Costakis must not return home until I tell you."

His great sincerity made an impression on me, as did the speed and assurance of his judgment.

15 November 1941

The Archbishop telephones to me regularly and always speaks briefly. "Costakis must not return."

18 November 1941

Today the Archbishop said to me laughingly on the telephone: "It's time to tell that husband of yours to get himself home."

Costakis is here again.

20 November 1941

Dr. Christos Karvounis[10] has come from Sparta. I was glad to see him. His every thought is about the resistance. He must be in touch with the Middle East Command.

From the outset this man impressed me. I came to know him one afternoon in the summer at the village of Vassaras on Mount Parnon.[11] We talked a great deal that evening. He was in agony over Greece. With mathematical precision, he considered all possible solutions. Organizations, rebellion, collaboration with Free Greece. And he always ended with the same questions. "How long will the war last? How long can the country stand it?" He had come up to Vassaras to visit a woman who was gravely ill in a neighboring village. Returning the next day, he knocked at the rickety door of our poor little cottage. But he was in bad shape, unshaven, pale from sleeplessness.

"All night I struggled in vain by her pillow, trying to save her," he said softly. And he went on talking, full of his impressions of the dead woman.

I gave him our only armchair, and served him some food from the kettle which hung in the fireplace.

"It must have been an exhausting night," I said, as if to myself, to give him a little time to pull himself together and get something into his stomach. "But when I think about death—the genuine tragic moment—I see it always as the separation of people who love each other. This woman had no one."

There was a long silence.

"We must go beyond that," he answered, as if continuing my thought. "Death is the only way we confront God. For this we need an innermost concentration—full, faithful, undivided. We must free ourselves from grief in order to give ourselves wholly to this innermost concentration."

He was silent again. Then, "Let me free man from pain that

---

[10] Christos Karvounis was a surgeon. He had studied eight years in Germany and had a private clinic in Sparta.

[11] Vassaras, the small village near Sparta where we stayed at the time of the German entry, temporary refugees from the bombing.

he may approach death in full consciousness of life, so that he may enter into the mystery of God," he continued quietly.

Soon the muleteer came with his animal to take the doctor back to Sparta. I did not see him again.

And today, here in my house, the same thought torments him: "How long will the war last? How long can the country stand it?"—as if he were the only Greek, the only one responsible.

22 November 1941

I sold my children's bicycle for a gold sovereign and went to Asyrmato[12] to buy beans. I wanted very much to find also some oil and an egg or two.

Some dirty, unshaven men took their hands out of their pockets and showed me, secretly, like dice in their fists, samples of fava beans and chickpeas. I loaded up with two okes of beans and two of peas and returned home.

25 November 1941

It is night. Cold, snow, hunger.

What will this hunger do to us? How shall we feed the starving children?

I had a most wonderful dream. A long, long table, covered with the most beautiful food and sweets. At the head sat the Christ Child and around Him the countless Greek children. All of them were eating with great appetite and delight, their faces smeared from ear to ear. Among them were many of my little friends, winking their eyes at me with joy.

I woke up with the feeling that I had just left Paradise, and, fully awake, I sank slowly into the familiar nightmare. My room is freezing cold. I am hungry. I never get up from the table satisfied. Around me gather all the little faces of Plaka, but as they really are, skeletons, all eyes. Eyes full of bewilderment, eyes that

---

[12] Suburb, center of the Black Market.

do not understand. What is there to understand? That the earth is dried up? That love is dried up? And there are so many of them. I have come to know them all during the months of the war. I have mobilized my friends to save for me every last crumb of food. And I do the same. They put whatever they have into tin cans and bring them to me. Then at twilight, with flashlight in hand, we seek out these children in the dark rooms of the old houses and divide up whatever we have.

Yesterday in the evening, at 10 Thucydides Street, little Stephanos was waiting alone, stretched out in a corner of the dilapidated room. He was waiting for us as he does every evening, with his eyes fixed on the door.

When you don't know about all this, perhaps you can find a little peace. But when you have a friendship with a child, a friendship which he gives you freely, when he believes in you, and doesn't seek you out, but just looks for you with his big eyes, and waits—God! There is no time for delay—not a day, not an hour. Something must be done. I pace up and down in my room, trying to get warm, then sit down again and write in order to fight the nightmares which gather 'round me.

26 November 1941

What shall we do about the mothers? I see them every day, and I am in despair. Their needs are so many, and what we offer is so little. Today again they all came to Byron Street.[13] Irene with her four children, and little Stratos, only two years old. Artemis, also with four children, the last two just babies. She weeps in desperation because they have reached the age of two and have lost their claim on milk from the Red Cross. Maria, whose husband died of tuberculosis at the Sanatorium of the Savior, her eyes full of pain and anguished concern for the health of her two little boys. Eleni, whose gallant son, twenty years old, died of a tumor, and now she trembles for the three younger ones. Sophia with her handsome boy, whom she constantly holds tight in her arms, as

[13] One of our offices was on Byron Street.

13

if this way she might save him from harm. Daphne, always spotless, with her three babies. And others, still others, countless others.

Oh God, let the children live! Let not one of them die!

1 December 1941

This morning in Byron Street a young man came looking for us with a child in his arms. We were terrified when we saw the little creature, his body covered with open sores. We recognized him immediately. We had been to their house. I remembered his mother, clean and beautiful, and this child and his little brother, always so well cared for.

"How did you let the child come to such a state?" I asked, frightened. Then the young man exploded. Was it anger? Was it sobbing? I don't know.

"She went away," he said. "She left her two children and disappeared." I realized that he was more tormented by suspicions of his wife's faithlessness than by his child's illness. But suddenly I felt sure that the young woman had committed suicide. Who knows by what means she killed herself? I remember her as such a tender mother, so proud. When I told him what I had in mind the man became thoughtful. We kept the child. We took him to the children's hospital.

2 December 1941

At last we succeeded in opening the Plaka canteen in Thucydides Street. We took on as cook Stella, a clean, honest woman from the quarter. She is good with the children. It makes her happy to fill up their plates again.

8 December 1941

The Germans have made a new law. "Anyone who hides one of the Allies will be shot."

They shot Panayiotis Charidis for having provided some English men with food. And they arrested Fotini Argyropoulou for having concealed the Australian, John Richardson.

The field of action narrows. But we have still many allies scattered about, hidden here and there. They get away as quickly as possible. The departures to Egypt continue and are more frequent.

Alexandra Poubourra worked splendidly. She herself went with our friends to the little port where the caique picked them up. But now they have arrested both Alexandra and her brother. In prison they are torturing them to make them reveal the names of the people they were working with. Merciless beating, burning with hot rods and lighted cigarettes. But not a single name escapes them.

9 December 1941

Another hard day. The Italians have arrested Katina Doussi. There is nothing about her to suggest that she is important. She is very poor and seems to be ill. Someone betrayed her.

15 December 1941

The news from the prison is not good. Katina is going through dark hours. Every day interrogations. Every day beatings. How much can the body endure? And over and over again they ask the same question: "Who helped you?" Katina puts on the most stupid air possible, and says, as if to herself, "I don't remember, my boy . . . I don't remember, my boy. . . ."

18 December 1941

Last time it was a superior Italian officer who interrogated Katina. He looked at her sharply, he shook her, he studied her, he asked her some questions, and finally concluded with certainty that the woman was pathologically stupid.

Sometimes we have a little luck.

20 December 1941

Today Lena and Alex came to see me. They have had a good idea: to launch a movement within the framework of the Archbishopric and to ask every Greek household to give a plate of food to a child who will be assigned to knock at the door each day at noon.[14] Immediately, with no delay, we organized the plan and asked to see the Archbishop.

21 December 1941

Christmas Eve. We have decided to forget the privation and the bitterness and to prepare a Christmas tree for the children of Plaka. Two rooms of the house have become a regular workshop. Despina and Dora, together with some of their classmates, are dyeing, sewing, gluing, renovating all their toys, both their own and those their friends have brought. I have given them all my scraps of material so that they can make little blankets and mattresses and doll clothes.

29 December 1941

Everything is ready. Under the tree the Christ Child in His crib is almost alive. In the dining room, the big table is opened out and loaded with toys. My friends have sent me sweets: a platter of kourabiedes, a large pitta, and honey macaroons. The house is full of children happy for the first time in many days. They eat the sweets and gaze at the toys. Despina and Dora and their friends, with the sure instinct of children, understand immediately their longings and try to satisfy them.

14 We called this movement "Life for the Child."

New Year's Eve. We closed the office in Byron Street late, and I started for home. I went ahead through the icy night. The darkness was thick. Here and there I heard something like weeping, like groaning. I imagined bony hands reaching out, searching for something which I was absolutely unable to give them. Nor is there the slightest cause for hope. The Germans are winning everywhere. And this hunger, like a mass extermination of the race, is killing us all.

I try to hurry home. But my flashlight has gone bad, and I am tangled up in obstacles . . . in a pit . . . in the trunk of a frozen tree. . . .

The story of the Ghinis, sad and unjust, is the very hallmark of slavery. The priest who supported them at their execution tells me about it—and weeps as he tells me.

Four brothers. Two married and two unmarried. One of them, the youngest, named Constantine, on his way home one day, found a German soldier's shirt. The wind had carried it from a camp nearby. He picked it up and went along, unsuspecting. On the way, a German, seeing the shirt in his hands, fell on him and began to beat him with his pistol, shouting at him in German. Constantine tried to explain how he had found the shirt quite by chance. They couldn't understand each other, and the Nazi dragged Constantine toward the German encampment.

Meanwhile, the other brothers came running. The eldest, a married man, in trying to free his younger brother, threw the German down and bruised him slightly. This was the whole crime.

They arrested all four. The two younger ones, Thanassis and Constantine, took the whole responsibility on themselves in the hope of saving their older brothers who had families.

So the two young men were condemned to death "because German blood was shed." So said the decision of their military court. The German blood was the Nazi soldier's momentary scratch.

The Archbishop asked for their pardon. It was refused because German blood was shed. He asked a second time, the answer was the same.

Until the last moment, Thanassis, about to die,[4] thinks only of Constantine in the next cell. The two brothers are put to death in the morning. Thanassis hears the volley which kills his brother, and in a few moments sees his fresh blood on the column to which he himself is tied. Tears scald his eyes. Why had not a bullet taken him on the Albanian front?

[4] According to the priest who was present.

1 April 1942

Panayiotis Kanellopoulos[5] and his wife left yesterday for Egypt. How much I wish for good news of them quickly! All these departures for the Middle East cause us great anxiety. Certainly many arrive there safely. But how many never arrive!

7 April 1942

We are terribly disturbed. Four days ago Michalis Akylas[6] attempted to get away. From the first moment of the occupation, this aviator-poet had but one thought in his mind. To reach Free Greece and fight for his country. Other officers went with him. They were unlucky and were all arrested. We tremble for their fate.

22 April 1942

Every day new bitterness poisons us. The Italians have arrested Aleko Zannas. I heard about it from his daughter Lena. Zannas, heroic and stout-hearted patriot, presides over the Distribution Committee of the Red Cross. Everybody trusts him. But he is ill. What will this trial do to him? Will he survive it?

27 May 1942

Yesterday the Nazis killed two wonderful young men, Angelos and Marinos Barkas. They were arrested at the very moment when they were cutting the German cables. I went to see their parents. We are almost neighbors. They live near St. John's Church in Vouliagmeni Street. Their mother keeps as a talisman a letter from her boys. She wept when she showed it to me.

[5] Professor of sociology, an eminent politician, later Prime Minister, and head of the nationalist party.
[6] Michalis Akylas, writer, Major in the Air Force.

30 May 1942

The Barkas parents came to see me. By now all the wives and mothers of those who were executed have found their way to our door. When in my ignorance I undertook to stand by them, I did not know what an endless Golgotha is compassion.

5 June 1942

Today is unbearable. Gone are the prewar times when the spirit could rejoice. Never again will we recover them. A bullet cut down Michalis Akylas. These Huns don't know who is standing before them and whom they are killing. They have killed not just the man but the rare spirit with which thousands of lives identify themselves.

And now around us, his bare words, his *Judas*, his *Socratic Dialogues*, serve as his dirge.

In our living room, still in the same place, is the armchair where he used to sit—analytical, simple, sincere.

6 June 1942

All these days, full of spring fragrance and deep sorrow, like an endless Good Friday. From his prison, Michalis Akylas says goodby to us with some stanzas. For any one living in our era, it is impossible to read them without weeping.

> *Here life has stopped*
> *in the vague half light*
> *of a far-off hope.*
>
> *All that we loved*
> *remained outside the door.*
> *We left it there*
> *when we crossed the threshold.*

There on the branches
of the garden trees
which soften the sombre aspect of the building
we have hung our longing, our love,
whatever else was ours.

There we have left
even ourselves—the selves we were then.

And we hoped for that day
when if it should come again
we would find perhaps what was but lately ours,
love, good fortune,
clear thinking,
and that divine simplicity
which goodness confers.

But before then,
before we step again over the threshold
of the iron gate,
how much will our bitter thought have
                    piled upon it . . . !

And ornaments are hung there,
and tempting toys
such as are put on Christmas trees.

But these have eyes which look at us tenderly,
but these have lips which smile at us,
and even little hearts which suffer.

Here life has stopped
In the vague half light
Of a far-off hope.

Time has passed
since separation
stood between us.

1942

Here life has stopped
in the vague half-light
of a far-off hope.

Michalis Akylas

10 January 1942

Yesterday a friend asked to see me.

"I come to ask you officially to join the EAM,"[1] he said. "They are asking for you by name."

"What is the EAM?" I asked. "Who is its leader?"

"The EAM is a resistance organization," he answered. "In times like these one doesn't mention names. I advise you to accept, otherwise they may think you are afraid."

I shrugged my shoulders. "I don't like to defend myself on moral grounds," I said to him. "If I do, it seems as if I were in some way accepting the accusation. But in any case, I have so much work that I haven't time for other responsibilities," and so I avoided accepting.

This morning the Archbishop asked for me. He wanted to increase the sum which we secretly give to the families of those who were executed. I spoke to him about the proposition of the EAM.

"But what is this EAM?" he said. "Can't they give us a name? I am in communication with Zervas,[2] with Psarros, with every intention or manifestation of resistance. I hear about this EAM, but I don't know it."

For a moment he was thoughtful.

"I don't believe in abstract ideas—at least for our country. I must know who are the men who are fighting for them. Only when the men are honorable do the ideas have substance. . . ."

He fell silent.

22 January 1942

George Kartalis[3] spends the evenings with us regularly. Yes-

---

[1] The national liberation front (EAM) organized by the Greek Communist party.

[2] Zervas, head of the resistance in Epirus.

[3] One of the most eminent politicians of our country, cultivated and courageous. He was minister before the war, minister during the liberation, and minister of co-ordination after the war, a volunteer in the war in 1940. He was one of the most important members in the committee of EKKA and a close collaborator with Colonel Psarros.

terday he spoke most sympathetically about Colonel Psarros and his resistance group in Macedonia.

3 February 1942

The atmosphere is heavy, unbearable. Gloom everywhere. Rommel is winning and advancing. London is bombed incessantly. There are rumors that the British will transfer their capital to some out-of-the-way place in the United Kingdom. Will this martyrdom, this humiliation, some day come to an end?

7 February 1942

Never have we been so cold. Inside and out, freezing. Dora's little hands are like sticks, when, in the evening, wrapped up like a cocoon, she shuts herself into the drawing room and tries to practice on the piano. It is colder in the house than it is in the street.

12 February 1942

"Life for the Child" is a blessing for those few small ones, nearly two thousand of them, who are to be found in the participating homes every day at noon. Most families, I'm sure, feel compassion for them and look after them as if they were their own.

Stella, the cook at the canteen, saves their noonday food, and gives it to them in the evening.

In spite of cold and hunger, the children of Plaka are in good health.

15 March 1942

Every day we are choked more and more by injustice. Every one fights in his own way.

And drops of rain hang on the closed door,
a cooling comfort, like diamonds
on shining rings
on fingers of light.

12 June 1942

I've spent hours with Evanthia Kalabouras. Her eyes, sunken like wells from weeping, gaze at me, expressionless. The day before yesterday the Nazis executed her son Yannis. Now they are after her other sons. The poor woman trembles, not knowing how to hide them. As for them, they want to join the resistance. The mountain, whichever one it may be, will swallow them too.

20 June 1942

I have seen Evanthia again. She has more courage now. So many children depend on her, and one is crippled. Her whole self is a prayer. What woman, what mother, bringing up human beings, does not measure how great is her love and how little her strength! Only by leaning on God can she hope and go on.

25 June 1942

Everything torments me. My house, which is as hot as a furnace. My two children, who are unmanageable from being so long shut up, and who don't know what to do with themselves. They clamber over the roof tiles with their friend Mika. They balance on the parapets of the terrace. I tremble for fear they will fall. But I don't dare confine them. The only breeze we have is up there.

10 July 1942

The Greek spirit has its own code. No Greek consents to give up his weapon. Three young Greeks have been executed for possessing arms. But nobody is afraid, nobody has given in, and every day there are new arrests for carrying weapons.

17 July 1942

The bond which ties us is so strong that each of us is a multiplied self. A poor woman in Adrianou Street fell gravely ill. We took her right off to a private hospital, and a distinguished surgeon operated on her. Today she is out of danger. All of my friends are helping.

30 July 1942

On the middle floor of our building my brother Angelos[7] is living through dramatic times. His wife, Roxane, was desperately tired, so she took her child and went to her father's house. Anxiety had shattered her nerves. Angelos sits curled up in an armchair, and tears run down his cheeks. Nor does he know that he is weeping. His ulcer has grown, and the pain is unbearable. Every so often he writes verses to his little boy. And he keeps looking for him, looking for him constantly, throughout the house. The doctor says that surgery is essential. We have decided to take him to the hospital.

15 August 1942

I am cheered by this regular contact with simple people. Perhaps love is the true road to justice.

---

[7] Angelos Seferiades with his wife, Roxane Papas, and their young son.

28 August 1942

Angelos' operation seemed endless. When they brought him from the surgery, he was shrunken and yellow on his hospital bed, as if at the point of death.

6 September 1942

Angelos' convalescence is very difficult. It goes slowly. However near I may be to him, he is alone. Roxane goes regularly to see him, but still he is alone. His eyes, staring indifferently at the sheets on his bed, build a white wall of loneliness around him.

10 September 1942

Yesterday George Kartalis brought home with him Apostolos Kapsalopoulos, a brave old officer with a lively intelligence. They had long talks with my husband about the formation of EKKA.[8] Costaki promised to help in every possible way.

15 September 1942

The Archbishop telephoned that Yannis Tsigantes[9] has arrived in Greece with big plans, plenty of money, and plenty of means. His first plan is the co-ordination of the resistance and its effective

[8] EKKA had a double purpose: national liberation with Colonel Psarros as the military leader and, later, social liberation, that is to say, greater social justice. At this moment, it had only one important objective: the organization of Psarros' regiment and its equipment by the British. Psarros was actually in Roumeli where he was trying with some officer friends to organize the 5/42 regiment of Evzones. At the beginning of the occupation he had attempted to train resistance groups in the mountains. During the first months his efforts extended as far as Macedonia.

[9] John Tsigantes, major in the infantry; head of a group sent from the Middle East to co-ordinate the Liberation Movement, to carry out sabotage, and to distribute relief to the families of victims.

co-operation with the Free Government. His arrival is an important event. We feel that Free Greece is taking us under its roof. We shall no longer be rivals, scattered, unorganized.

16 September 1942

Angelos has left the hospital. He is as weak as a thread and takes nourishment only with effort. Back in his own home, he lies motionless on his bed. We have a rare friend, Sister Semi, who looks after him.

19 September 1942

A mystery. Angelos' apartment is empty. Something bad has happened to him. Where can so sick a man be? I went around everywhere, asking quietly and looking for him. To the police, to the doors of the German and Italian offices. At the Commando Piazza, the carabinieri guard told me that a very feeble, dark-complexioned man had gone inside.

How long it takes this night to come to an end!

20 September 1942

This morning again Roxane and I asked everywhere. One man sent us to another. Finally, after great effort, we succeeded in getting the information that he is in Averoff Prison and that there is a serious charge against him.

21 September 1942

I tried immediately to reach Angelos in jail. Katina Doussi was a great help. It is a comfort to be able to take his noon meal to him.

When it is hard for me to do this, poor Katina takes it. Because she was kept there for months, she knows the jail like the inside of her pocket.

22 September 1942

These days the best people are to be found in Averoff Prison—some important officers and many other excellent Greeks. They amuse themselves as best they can and make it a point of honor to show no annoyance over their detention. They take even better care of themselves than they did before and are always in good humor. In the morning, newly shaven, with fresh linen, they sit chatting and smoking, and might almost be at the Club. And the carabinieri look at them respectfully.

23 September 1942

Along with his food, I send Angelos whatever else he needs. We can exchange ideas about all sorts of little things. Thank God he begins to eat better. On Sunday at eleven o'clock, I went with his little boy and stood outside the prison, so that he saw us from a distance.

But I cannot feel at ease about him. What will they accuse him of?

30 September 1942

When Katina came back, in her hand she had Angelos' package, unopened, just as I had given it to her. I looked at her, not understanding. My blood froze. "He isn't at Averoff any longer," she said. "They transferred him in handcuffs to Lamia, along with Colonel Papakyriazis."

Sick at heart, I lay down on my bed.

2 October 1942

George Kartalis is a great help to us. He is Angelos' friend, and he knows the Lamia area well. He immediately found a way to make contact with him.

3 October 1942

Kyrá Getsali came to see me. Six days ago, on September 27, the Italians executed her son Pericles, also a man named Lelos. The charge again was "carrying weapons."

Kyrá Getsali is from Chimarra. She had five sons. Three fell in the Albanian War. One is prisoner in Italy, and the last one, Pericles, belonged to the Rural Police. He and the two old people tried by every means to feed the four orphans whom the dead brothers left behind. Naturally, Pericles had not turned over his weapons. The same was true of his associate Lelos, also of the Rural Police.

One evening, Italian soldiers enter the estate to steal grapes. Pericles and Lelos stop them. But there are many Italians and they try to disarm our men. Under no circumstances will Pericles give up his gun. He comes to grips with the Italians who are trying to take it away from him. Things get rough. Pericles fights with everyone to save his pistol. And when he gets desperate, he fires and kills one of the Italians.

They sentence the two of them, both Pericles and Lelos, to death.

But Kyrá Getsali is a woman of true gallantry. Tall, erect, immaculate, she wears her black headdress, neatly and tightly bound to her head, like a crown.

She did not complain, she did not mourn. Only her breath came more rapidly when she spoke of her son.

"My sons always stood up like men. This was their obligation. It could not be otherwise. Their weapon was their valor, their freedom. How could they give it up? By chance it was an evil hour, and disaster fell on them."

I looked at her. I listened to her. I marveled at her. Grief had furrowed her aged face. But her nobility was great.

10 October 1942

All contact with Angelos has stopped. We are at the mercy of God. It appears that a battle will take place in the outskirts of Lamia. There are accusations against someone named Seferiades. What will come of this no one knows.

15 October 1942

Captain Stephen Doukas is, among others, a liaison agent for Tsigantes. He comes regularly to see my husband. Tsigantes wants to organize the Supreme National Council under the presidency of the Archbishop. It is difficult. They need people of prestige who are absolutely trustworthy. Costakis is giving names and ideas to Doukas who then sends them to Tsigantis.

2 November 1942

The doorbell rings incessantly, persistently—a well-known tune. I run to open the door. Unbelievable. There, in the frame of the door, Angelos with his knapsack. He sits down, loaded as he is, on the first chair he comes to. He talks, and I ply him with questions, and he tries to answer, and the words get all tangled up. He was brought before the prosecutor, and they were persuaded that he was not the Seferiades they were looking for.

Never mind how. He is here, and he is well. I look at him, I touch him, and I cannot believe my eyes. He speaks of Colonel Papakyriazis. "A brother," he calls him. "They bound us with the same handcuffs when they transferred us to Lamia. And we were not separated there. We were in the same cell. I left him my pallet and whatever else I had that he could make use of. What would I not give to have him here with me, free, as I am!"

5 November 1942

The house is transformed with Angelos' return. As if we had escaped from a heavy sorrow. He too has recovered his good humor. The children laugh as they look after him. Even the pessimistic Costakis makes jokes.

16 November 1942

The day before yesterday the Nazis shot Boukas, and today, Yannis Mastoris. In spite of the grave charges in the military court we always had a hope. Boukas was the first radio-telegrapher in the service of the Allies. He was arrested in 1941. At his trial they cited the numbers of submarines lost on his account. Mastoris had a transmitter. At least these brave men sold their lives dearly.

23 November 1942

The exchange between Tsigantis and Costakis continues. They have agreed on all the main points. The time has now come for them to meet with the Archbishop.

25 November 1942

Costakis' friends are meeting again here at home. The group meets regularly and discusses the postwar political developments. All of them are old acquaintances, and most of them are our good friends. Today for the first time came a Macedonian named Costas Karamanlis.[10] He spoke little, but what he said was to the point.

[10] Prime Minister of Greece, October 1955 to June 1963.

I was impressed with his judgment and his sincerity. I'm going to ask Costakis to invite him one day by himself so that I can come to know him better.

26 November 1942

Yesterday the bridge at Gorgopotamos was blown up. They say British parachutists dropped down and did the job together with some of our own men. But we really know nothing of the details. For certain we know only that the bridge was blown up, and we are greatly relieved. At least Rommel's reinforcements will not pass through Greece.

5 December 1942

In reprisal for Gorgopotamos, the Italians are executing hostages at Lamia. Colonel Papakyriazis is said to be among the dead. I am afraid it is the truth. How I wish I might never learn it!

I went down to Angelos' room. His head on his arms, he was bent over his desk. I realized that he knew about his friend before I did. I stroked his hair. He raised his head. He was in tears. "As it is with him, so it might have been with me," he said. "Every day we are playing dice with destiny."

6 December 1942

The blowing up of ESPO[11] was a deliverance for us as it was a shock and a scare for the Nazis. The patriots who undertook it purged the nation of a group-treason. They were among our best

---

[11] ESPO, the so-called Greek Patriotic Socialist Organization, had been founded by the Germans. It sought to enlist fools and organize them into a Greek regiment to fight beside the Nazis against Russia. Perrikos and his friends dynamited the ESPO offices, and some Germans were killed.

young men: the aviator, Perrikos, leader of PEAN,[12] and his friends; Mytilinaios, and Biba, the young girl, among others— the guardians of our honor, since we no longer have any soil to guard.

12 December 1942

The Germans arrested all those who were responsible and many others who had nothing to do with the ESPO affair. When at night we lie down in our own beds, we thank God.

20 December 1942

In the midst of our agony some good news. Mytilinaios escaped from prison. He had great muscular strength, so that he managed to bend the iron bars and pass through the window into the next room. It was empty, except for a German overcoat and a cap. He put them on and went out quietly.

31 December 1942

I stand opposite Parnassos[13] by the wall of St. George's Church. The trial over the ESPO explosion has come to an end. They are bringing out the condemned.

Many people are still waiting outside.

Perrikos was sentenced to death. During the interrogation, he behaved responsibly and bravely, just as he had during the action itself. To the very end, he tried to persuade the Germans that he had brought off the explosion all by himself. Under torture, the girl confessed that she too helped.

[12] Constantine Perrikos, officer in the Air Force, had founded with his companions the PEAN (Panhellenic Union of Young Fighters).
[13] The German Military Court was set up in Parnassos Hall.

Time passes. Some people talk, some weep. The crowd thins out, dissolves. In the cold mist, everything is blurred. There on the sidewalk, petrified, like a charred statue, Perrikos' wife, with her little ones.

1943

Fate snatched from you
The victor's laurel bough,
And wove for you
Another wreath instead,
Of myrtle
And the mourning cypress.

. . . .

But when he nears
The earth wherein you lie,
Time will change course
In reverence
For that honored soil.

Calvos, To the Sacred Legion

7 January 1943

They hunt us down without ceasing. Every day they kill. On the eve of Epiphany, the Germans shot Demetrius Yannatos and two officers. They also condemned Costas Yannatos. But he went mad, and they have committed him to the insane asylum.[1]

This morning they executed hostages, twenty patriotic Greeks whose names they do not give out, nor do they turn over the bodies for burial. Sleet has been falling since morning. Who, one wonders, are the slain? Each one trembles for his own.

I went to the Archbishop's headquarters. Many people there. All the doors open. Women sobbing.

The Archbishop looks gloomily through various watches, keys, purses scattered on his desk. All that remains of those who are gone. The silence is oppressive.

And to think that this very evening was the one my husband had arranged for the meeting of the Archbishop and Tsigantes at our home!

8 January 1943

Ravaged, exhausted, the Archbishop came late yesterday to our house where Tsigantes was waiting for him. The scenes he had lived through all day were still with him, tormenting him.

Gradually he began to speak, and this gave him some relief, some outlet. Afterward he and Tsigantes and Costakis laid the foundations for the National Council.

12 January 1943

My husband went to meet Tsigantes in a house behind the Perroquet Theatre. They still had much to discuss. Two of Tsigantes' collaborators were also present.

[1] Because he had been arrested and cruelly tortured in 1942, we believed in the madness of Dr. Costas Yannatos, but after the departure of the Germans he was all right, and we learned that his insanity had been feigned.

13 January 1943

Tragic hours at the third Cemetery. After many attempts the Archbishop finally got permission to open the common grave of those who were executed on January 7.

He stood erect, the only responsible person among all those desperate people, and gave the order for the exhuming.

Under the fine icy rain, in the midst of tears, the dead were identified by their relatives. For each a fervent common prayer, and a grave of his own.

14 January 1943

Incredible as fiction. Stephen Doukas, harrowed by grief, brought us the news. Tsigantes is dead. A woman—they say she was jealous—telephoned the Italians:

"Go to Patission 86. You will arrest an Englishman."

The Italians laid seige to the apartment building. It was a real battle.

15 January 1943

His funeral took place today. We buried the gallant fighter, buried too the idea of a Pan-Hellenic resistance. Stephen came in the evening and brought us more news. After receiving the phone call, the Italians began a systematic search of every floor of the building. In Tsigantes' suite there were two of our officers. When they tried to leave, they were prevented by the Italian guard. They went back and told Tsigantes that he was besieged. With utter *sang froid* he began to burn his records. There were many. There wasn't time to burn them all. He tore them up and threw the pieces into the fire. He threw them also into the toilet bowl. The Italians saw the smoke and broke into the suite. Tsigantes took out his pistol, shot at the Italian, and tried to flee. But at the outer door the sentry stopped him. Tsigantes fired at him too and wounded him. But the wounded man drew on him from behind, and Tsigantes fell dead.

24 January 1943

Very many officers and citizens are mixed up in the Tsigantes affairs. During all those months he spent in Greece he had made endless contacts. Since Tsigantes was accustomed to keep notes, no one knows at this moment whether or not his own name is in the hands of the Italians.

Everyone is in hiding. Stephen Doukas is in touch with a network of counterespionage. He passes by the house regularly and gives me the latest news. I in turn transmit it to Costakis, and he to the Archbishop. The Italians broke open the toilet bowl and have lots of papers in their possession.

4 February 1943

Today they executed Constantine Perrikos. I read the justification of the verdict to condemn him: "Illegal carrying of arms, possession of explosive materials, writing and distribution of printed propaganda, organization of a hostile faction to incite strikes and demonstrations against the Germans." They write down only what they found out. And there is so much that they never found out.[2]

How much we wanted to save Perrikos! How we prayed for him! The Archbishop saw the military authorities, and saw them again, but they were obdurate. As he died, he said to the Germans, "I am a Greek officer. I did my duty." And they gave him a military salute.

[2] Perrikos' work went on until the liberation. PEAN organized fighting units which it succeeded in equipping, training, and putting at the disposal of the military commander of Attica.

Along with the volley, his voice was heard: "Long live Greece!"
Long live Greece—a phrase worn from much use, but at that
moment it rang out like the living soul of the nation.

7 February 1943

" 'What's the matter, my child? You look thoughtful, pale.' "
" 'Nothing, Mama. I'll just stay home for a day to rest a little.' "
"He didn't go to work. How was I, ill-fated woman that I am,
to know what my brave son had in his head?"
So spoke the mother of Elias Alevizakis in utter misery.
For some days a dark foreboding had prevailed in the Malt-
simiotis factory the Germans have requisitioned. They were much
disturbed. The airplane motors the factory was building were not
working properly.
Elias and two co-workers went to work mornings, their mouths
full of metal filings. These filings they would blow into the
engines of the planes. The planes either fell or didn't start at all.
The motors were destroyed.
The Germans searched persistently to find out what was wrong.
They dismantled more than thirty motors to make sure that they
found the same metal filings in all of them. Alevizakis knew that
they would seize him, and he could have fled. But he loved his
mother. He adored her, and he felt for her. He saw how, every
day, beginning at dawn, she struggled alone for his younger
brothers and sisters. He was afraid that something bad would
happen to her. For a few days he pretended to be ill. But when
they came to arrest him, he surrendered. The trial of the three
men took place on the 5th of February, in front of the whole personnel of the factory, so as to make an example of them. The
verdict was declared final the same day. Yesterday morning they
were shot.
All these executions leave many without protection. From the
one yesterday, Alevizakis' mother is left alone with five small
children; Ioannides left his wife, his child, his mother, his sister,
and a brother with frostbitten feet; Barkados left a sick mother.

8 February 1943

Now the cup runs over. There are all these homes in mourning—and every day more of them, and they simply cannot live with the little help we give them secretly from the Archbishop. The Red Cross helps too, but this aid is very meager. We must do something, we who are still alive. We must guarantee these families some economic security so that they can live with dignity and honor. With the honor which the fulless of their gift demands.

10 February 1943

The Archbishop has made an important decision which he has been working over for some time. Today he is announcing a Pan-Hellenic Fund for the imprisoned and their families.

11 February 1943

The day before yesterday in the Italian military court Aleko Zannas' trial began. I have seen his daughter Lena. She is utterly distressed and weary.

16 February 1943

We are following the Zannas trial in agony. It involves the famous Atkinson affair. It dates from 1941, and that is why Zannas is in jail. The English officer, John Atkinson, stayed behind in Greece at the time of the invasion and was later helped by Greeks to escape to the Middle East. He asked the British Command to use him for missions to Greece, so he came back again to Athens. He asked to be put in touch with Zannas. They met one evening in 1941 and discussed many things related to plans for the escape of the British and the supply lines. Atkinson left and then returned again, this time to Anti-Paros. There the lawyer Tzavellas had a big estate. The Allied submarines would put in at his little port and all the people who came and went to the Middle East would gather at his house. Tzavellas received Italians too, so as to throw ashes in their eyes. To this harbor a submarine brought Atkinson in mufti. He had a valise in his hand. Kypriadis[3] accompanied him with wireless equipment. There must have been some betrayal because the Italian lieutenant at Paros received an order from his superior at Syra to search Tzavellas' house. The lieutenant laughed at the order: a short time before he had been eating there with other carabinieri. But he went back. He and his men heard noise and conversation. They tried to open the door. It wouldn't open. They threw a hand grenade, and the door fell down. Inside, Atkinson, wounded in the leg by the grenade, tried to fight back and killed the Italian lieutenant. Kypriadis had the presence of mind to seize the valise and the wireless and disappear. He destroyed his code book, whatever papers he had, and the wireless. Not knowing the contents of the valise, he gave it to a peasant, just as it was, unopened, either to be hidden or destroyed. The peasant threw it into a ravine, and the wounded Atkinson hid himself in the bushes.

Next day the Italians searched the whole area and found the valise. In it were five hundred gold sovereigns, ten thousand dollars, and a report to Eden on the subject of the supply lines, also a note that Zannas had given them all the information. Atkinson, himself wounded and without food, surrendered. With Tzavellas, his wife, his father, Kypriadis, and two local boatmen, he was taken to the Averoff Prison.

24 February 1943

The verdict of the Italian court martial on the Anti-Paros affair has come out. Surely we have paid dearly for this action. First of all, with the lives of so many of our own people. Yesterday

[3] His real name was Arvanitopoulos, radio-telegraph operator. He was arrested and condemned to death under his pseudonym, Kypriadis. To save his family, he had succeeded in convincing the Italians that he was from Cyprus and knew no one in Greece.

they shot Tzavellas and Kypriadis, brave, well-organized patriots. Their services were beyond price. They also shot the two courageous young boatmen who had transported all the people Tzavellas helped to escape on the Allied submarine.

The tribulations of Aleko Zannas are not over: sick for a year in jail, and now condemned to go as a prisoner to Italy.

And we paid also with the sinking of the British submarine which brought Atkinson to Greece.

25 February 1943

Poor Mrs. Tzavellas, now a widow, her heart in mourning, is going back to her babies. For a year now while she was in jail she had left them to God's mercy.

26 February 1943

By the way he faced death, Elias Kanaris revived the whole spirit of Ancient Greece. They killed him the day before yesterday, but because of him, slavery lost some of its burden. Not because he is braver than other brave men, but because he embraces the hard hour with such spirit that the enemy stands powerless before him. Without being aware of it, he thinks like Socrates. They cannot harm him, they can only kill him.[4] He plays the game of death and war with dash. Like Odysseus, he uses his great and small virtues to the limit—his presence of mind, his cunning, his manly courage, his physical strength—and he gets pleasure out of them.

Elias Kanaris was a mechanic from Smyrna. The first year of our slavery he organized departures to Egypt. In April 1942, the Germans seized him and imprisoned him in the Averoff. When

[4] *Apology of Socrates* 30 C–D. "Neither Meletus nor Anytus can do me any harm at all; they would not have the power, because I do not believe that the law of God permits a better man to be harmed by a worse." (Treddenick)

the interrogations began, they asked him to show them the place from which the caiques took off. Kanaris agreed. They gave him an escort of seven men from the Gestapo. He took them to the village of Vathi near Chalkis, according to an arrangement he had made from prison with one of his friends. Pointing out to the Germans his friend's house, he said to them:

"There is a transmitter in there. Let six of you watch outside in case the wireless operator tries to get away, and I will go in with one of you to seize him." The moment they entered the house, Kanaris and his friend gagged and bound the German, and disarmed him. Then they escaped by a small window which looked in the opposite direction.

For seven months Kanaris hid in the area of Chalkis, and the Nazis searched for him madly in the most unlikely places. At last they caught him for the second time, condemned him, and, on February 24, they executed him. They gave him a heavy sentence: three times to death and three years in jail. But the sentence filled him with pride. He wrote to his friends: "I, Elias Kanaris, write to you—champion and record-holder among those about to die." He wrote to his brother, disabled on the Albanian front: "Brother, among all those they have executed up until to-day, they have accused me of more things than anybody else. I've broken the record. I laugh as I write to you. And you mustn't mourn for me. I want you to invite your friends, give them a dinner, read them my letter, and drink to the repose of my soul. I don't want any weeping. I want you to behave like men and like Greeks. I am dying for my country."

But the point at which his brave spirit faltered a little was when he wrote to his little son, two years old: "Costa my boy, I want you to forgive me for leaving you an orphan when you are so young. I want you to pray for me. And, my boy, don't ever play cards, and don't ever injure a woman. In all your life, be honest and sincere. Love your country and be a good Christian. My boy, I am dying like a man with your name on my lips. My son, my little one, forgive me that I am leaving you an orphan. . . ."

Yesterday this child of two years came to me with his grandmother because his mother is sick. He cannot understand now what a great legacy his father left him.

28 February 1943

Last night we had unthinkable news. Inconceivable news. The aged Palamas[5] is dead. We had forgotten that he was mortal. We hurried immediately to Periander Street. Sikelianos[6] was already there, he too overcome with emotion. Not a breath was heard. Speechless, we all looked at the old man, lying as if asleep, and we stood for a long time, waiting, beside him. What were we waiting for? Perhaps for the familiar sparkle of his eyes under his bushy brows . . . But no more . . . The aura spread. A great soul, plunging toward Hades, shakes the world, and makes it one. . . .

How did all of Athens learn of his death, and seethe with the news? How did the cemetery come to be black with people? All of Greece was there. The Italian guards gathered in their corners and looked on, wondering, frightened. The silent crowd had a grandeur that made the foreigners wary. It was sharing in the death.

With effort we pushed into the church. Thousands remained outside. The Archbishop conducted the service, and bade farewell to the dead man. Then there came a voice which shook the roof and the walls, the voice of Sikelianos:

> *"At this bier, Greece bows"*
>
> . . . .
>
> *"Let the trumpets sound . . ."*

Young men lifted the bier, and, led by Sikelianos, they bore him out into the sunlight and the boundless throng. All of us had left our bodies behind and were marching forward with the dead

---

[5] Our great poet, Costis Palamas (1859–1943)
[6] Another great poet, Angelos Sikelianos (1884–1951)

man. Beside me, Katsimbalis[7] and Costakis were pale with emotion.

The great moment came. We heard the first earth fall upon the wood. Then Katsimbalis with the strongest voice of all began the hymn:

"I know you from the sword's fierce edge. . . ."[8] and we all joined in.

The Greek earth was calm. We had achieved it by other roads. We were free.

2 March 1943

Athens buzzes with a nightmarish rumor. Civilian conscription. The order has come from Berlin. All young Greeks will be sent to Germany to work. The newspaper, *German News for Greece,* states it clearly. Fear and terror in all our hearts. Every evening our house is full of people we know, and others whom we do not. All are asking to go to the mountains. We are in regular communication with EKKA, with Kartalis and Kapsalopoulos, and they in turn with Psarros. His regiment of Evzones is now a battle-ready military unit. The Middle East Command has recognized it and is going to equip it. We want to send as many as we can to Colonel Psarros, but it is not easy, and it is certainly not possible to send them all. Every young man is suspect.

The city is in a state of great excitement. Demonstrations in the streets, strikes, a fire at the Ministry of Labor. The Italians and Germans shoot at the crowds. Many are killed. Since the 25th, the telephone service has been on strike, in spite of the fact that it is considered a military service. The school children are striking too.

And a great Pan-Hellenic strike has been proclaimed.

[7] George Katsimbalis, an exceptional personality of our era. Man of letters, critic, and hero of Henry Miller's book, *The Colossus of Maroussi.* Whoever does not know him cannot fully comprehend the literary world of our time.

[8] From *Ode to Liberty* by Dionysios Solomos (1798–1857). The first stanzas, set to music by Manzaros, became the national anthem of Greece.

The Archbishop, like a tall mast in this wild sea of humanity, has made his decision. On the seventh of March, if the order has not been recalled, he himself will lead a march through the streets of Athens—all the organizations and all the strikers—while the bells toll mournfully. But before then, as soon as possible, he must have a conference with the Germans. He has asked to see Altenburg. They have set a time, Saturday evening, the sixth of March. It will be the last night of Carnival. Our agony has reached a peak.

7 March 1943

Sunday. How joyfully the cathedral bells are ringing! The morning papers announce the great news. The order for civilian conscription in Greece has been recalled.

My husband and I went to Psychiko to see the Archbishop. Last night he had his first attack of angina. He was in bed and spoke with effort. He told us what had happened the evening before at the German Embassy. With firmness he made plain to the German plenipotentiary the utter desperation of the Greek people and his own decision to arouse the crowds.

"But then," said Altenburg, "I shall be obliged to arrest you. You would be leading a revolt."

The Archbishop, cool, patient, without adding anything more, asked again for the recall of the order. It was not within the province of the plenipotentiary to answer. He telephoned to Thessalonika. Nor had Thessalonika the authority to recall the order. He telephoned to Berlin. Hours passed. Because we have martial law, the Archbishop's car had to leave. He continued to sit on an embassy chair, leaning his head on his crosier. Finally, at three in the morning, Berlin answered that it agreed to recall the order for civilian conscription in Greece.

Immediately the communique was given to the morning papers so that they could announce the good news. The people's anxiety was not to be prolonged.

At the German Embassy they were celebrating the last night of

Carnival. A German woman, drunk and loaded down with flowers, was returning home at that very time.

"They obliged me to ride wth her," the Archbishop said, very tired. "One more humilitation."

15 March 1943

The Archbishop's Fund has been very successful. He is organizing two services. One for those in prison and their families, the other for the families of those who have been executed.

24 March 1943

The Archbishop sent for me. "At last I want to ask you to undertake officially the service for the protection of the families of the executed," he said. "What you were doing before, secretly and meagerly, you must now do openly and abundantly. These families must lack nothing. Money, clothing, medical care —they must have them all. As if their men were still alive—and even better. Furthermore, I want us to extend it to all of Greece. The families of those executed in the provinces must have their allowances. The bishops will bring you lists of their names, and it will be for you to give them sufficient funds. The Greeks must live."[9]

[9] This letter from the wife of Yatrakis, received toward the end of 1943, shows how necessary the service was:
"Please read.
"We lived in Piraeus before the war. My husband was denounced and accused of equipping resistance forces. The Germans were searching for him so that we had to go away to Crete. There, the German commander again searched for us; a Greek policeman came, he warned my husband and said to him, 'The Germans have given me a warrant for your arrest. But hide if you can, and take to the mountains.' So that's what he did. He left and took to the mountains. A week later it was my turn and they went after me so that I had to go to the mountains with my children. I stayed there four months. Then my baby fell ill with a temperature of 104 degrees. I was forced to go down to Canea. I was there hardly three days when they arrested me, put me in prison with my two children, and the baby

52

26 March 1943

I saw Lilika Theotokas.[10] She is an exceptional woman. Under the auspices of the Red Cross, she and her volunteers wholeheartedly do all they can for the survivors of the executed. We came to an understanding immediately. All of us will work together.

27 March 1943

Things are going well, but there is no room at the Archbishop's headquarters. The first floor is at the disposal of the Fund Committee and the service for those who are detained. The Archbishop's secretary will have to give us the little room next to his on the second floor. It is the only one empty.

30 March 1943

Our little office is quite adequate. We work together in confidence and affection. All are splendid people. My only request is

---

with 104 degrees temperature. I stayed there 20 days subjected to torture which one can't write or tell, in order to make me say where my husband was and why he went to the mountains. When he learned that they were putting such pressure on me, he felt he had to appear. No sooner did he do so than he went to prison. They took my husband and his companions to the drill ground, and gave them shovels and mattocks for digging their graves. Then they made them stand at attention, and the Nazi asked them if they wanted to say a last word to their children and families. Then he said, 'Fire!' and they opened fire with machine guns, killing 25 men.

"When they had been killed, I suffered total loss of speech. They took me to a hospital where I stayed 48 hours. I came to myself and went home.

"I had to go to Piraeus because my brother was in the mountains, and I hadn't a penny. I stayed with a cousin. After 15 days she told me to look for a room, because I had neither money, nor clothes, nor anything. I went to the Red Cross and they sent me to you. With the money you gave me, I have been able to live till now.

"I thank you very much." Panayota Yatrakis.

[10] Sister of the writer George Theotokas, she became the wife of Constantine Alevizatos, professor of medicine at the University.

that we should have as treasurer an employee of the bank. When funds are being dispensed, all these formalities are necessary.

4 April 1943

Every morning now I am in my office at nine. Many people come there. Anyone in trouble comes to see us.

5 April 1943

The Italian chargé d'affaires, Chigi, visited the Archbishop and protested vigorously about our service. They called me in to serve as interpreter. "This service of yours," he said, "very much annoys the military authorities. They carry out executions in order to frighten people. When the Greeks know that their families are insured against privation, they will be still more brave."

"Do you want Christ's Church to leave all these orphans unprotected?" asked the Archbishop in his most monk-like manner. And immediately he changed the subject, asking the release of more oil. Chigi then spoke more urgently.

"But then why don't you look after the families of the men from the Security Battalions, those whom the Communists kill? Why don't you take a position against communism, you who are of the ruling class?" I translated his words to the Archbishop. "Tell him," he answered, "that he may be a great diplomat, but that I wouldn't take him even as a candle-lighter." I turned toward Chigi, trying to keep a straight face. I knew exactly what the Archbishop was thinking, and took it on myself to say to Chigi, "When you go away, your excellency, we will take a position. At present in this country, there are for us only Greeks against foreigners. This is also our basic difference with the Communists."

6 April 1943

On the first floor of the Archbishop's headquarters we have a storeroom for clothing, blankets, food. I never think about the future, since every hour may be our last. For this reason nobody in need appears without receiving help that very moment. The storeroom becomes empty, but it fills up again with new donations.

8 April 1943

Every day at our office the most unlikely, the most urgent problems turn up. Guerrilla fighters come from Zervas, from Psarros. They want to go back to the mountains and haven't the means to do so. The Middle East Command asks information about the resistance groups. Young people want to offer their services without having to leave their homes. And it is right that they should not be left out of the universal spirit of resistance. City and Rural Police who have been dismissed must be given help. It is up to us to find solutions for all these problems without compromising the Archbishop. There are traitors everywhere.

10 April 1943

The Archbishop is no bureaucrat. What interests him is to rescue as many souls as he can from chaos.

He thinks it is a good thing to publicize the Fund for Those Who Are Detained. And he is right. Publicity will reduce suspicion.

12 April 1943

Today at the office we discussed putting on a benefit for the Fund. It is the best way to give it publicity. We will have it at the "Olympia," and ask Rena Kyriakou to play the piano for us.

13 April 1943

We have organized the committee for the benefit from among the leading women of Athens. They are all very eager.

Already people are beginning to reserve seats at the "Olympia." We expect an enormous crowd.

17 April 1943

These days another pressing problem occupies the Archbishop. The Jews.

The evil intentions of the Nazis are evident. Since the beginning of the year, they have been taking a census. Then the order came for every Jew who is not a Greek subject to return to his country, and for all the Greek Jews to go with their families to Poland. This last news was overwhelming.

The Archbishop simply cannot abandon human beings to torture. He took all possible steps with the German plenipotentiary. Naturally these efforts came to nothing. The Nazis long since drew up their policy. And now the tragic persecution of the Jews has begun. The Archbishop is trying to relieve their suffering, to break down their isolation. He has asked the Red Cross to organize canteens for them.

20 April 1943

In absolute secrecy, we are baptizing Jews. At great personal risk the Archbishop is making enormous efforts to save as many Jews as he can. He has come to an understanding with the Mayor's office in Athens. A special registry has been opened, and, after baptism, these people are given certificates which say that they are Greek Christians.

21 April 1943

Finally, after so long a delay, the aid for which we waited has come to Colonel Psarros. On the 16th of April, the Allies dropped to his regiment munitions, arms, wireless equipment, clothing, and four English officers under command of Captain Jeff.

25 April 1943

Why were the doorbells ringing, both up and down stairs? I myself went to answer. There were two German officers and one Greek. The latter had in his hands a roll of wire.

"We want the house," the Greek said straight out. They came in and went through the drawing rooms and the bedrooms as if they owned the place. I followed them, not really grasping what it all meant. They went up on the terrace. The officer with the wire fastened one end of it to a column and tossed the rest across to the terrace of the next house, which was also being requisitioned. They seemed pleased. The little garden delighted them. They told me they would come back in the afternoon with the others and went away.

I stood there like a pillar of salt. What could we do now? What things would I take? Where would I take them? And on the floor below us there was also my father's home, full of valuable objects, like a museum.

Both my head and my heart are empty.

Sometimes we women have an upside-down sense of values. There is war, slavery, death—but home is home. Without it we are naked, beggars.

What can I do? I'm in despair.

I fall on my knees before Panayia. With Christ she holds my heart in her hands.

At noon I did not eat. I had a bad headache. I felt as if I had had a concussion. I lay down for a moment, and I must have dropped off to sleep. Because I had a dream. What held me to the hard, solid earth had been broken. I was alone in a powerful, roaring wind. As I stood trembling in the dark space, You came, Great Shade, to help me. And I saw an army, a vast army, marching on Kydathineon Street. But a woman with dark robes opened her arms and blocked the street. Her arms and her robes became an impenetrable wall. No one could enter.

I got up from my bed heavily, and, with effort, I went again to my knees before Her ikon with a sweet, an infinite confidence.

The men did not appear again. And within me I have a sure feeling that they will not.

28 April 1943

Our office is full of dirges.

A woman from Kymi, Kyrá Chartsa, fell to her knees in the middle of the room and lamented for her two slain sons as if their bodies were there before her. She sang of their valor, she sang the lullabies which she had sung to them when they were babies. She was unaware of the people around her. And none of us dared to interrupt her. When at last she paused, we gave her water and helped her to a chair. She started to tell us her story. Every now and then dark images crossed her mind, and she broke out again in lamentation.

Allied planes had dropped weapons at Kymi, and the young Chartsa brothers had picked them up and hidden them. But the Fascists were lying in wait for them. They killed the boys and buried them before their mother's eyes.

We tried to comfort her. To give her a little strength. But what comfort can there be for the mother who sees open before her the grave of her sons?

We tried to relieve her of material cares, to give a little warmth to her loneliness. We gave money and promised to send her some every month. We gave her food and clothing. We told her that whatever she wants, we will always stay by her. But she didn't know what to do with herself. She was empty.

She went away a little calmer. She is going back to Kymi.

5 May 1943

Kyrá Chartsa must have talked too much to her neighbors in Kymi. At the Office I received a personal summons to appear at the Commando Piazza.

Lots of people tell me not to go. And perhaps I would consider not going if the summons had come to my house. But it came to the Archbishop's headquarters. I have an obligation to appear.

After my brother's imprisonment, I am almost certain they will send me to jail. I think of my children in this chaos of the occupation. I think of my husband. They have a dossier on him and he has to stay in hiding. Who knows how long he will be at liberty and alive? Times are very hard.

6 May 1943

I must appear at five this afternoon. I haven't much time. I called a good friend who suffers from heart trouble and leads a quiet life. Her little girl, Mika, is a close friend to my daughters. I gave her all the money I had and begged her, if I should not return, to look after the children.

6 May 1943

Evening. With God's help, we have won this difficult day. My mind is confused, but I want to set down all that I remember clearly.

This afternoon I placed a few necessary things in a bag and put on my red coat to help keep up my spirits. At the door little Despina asked me, her eyes full of tears, "Mummy, will you be late?" The child must have guessed something. I turned and looked at her. For me at that moment, the whole world was there in those big eyes of hers, fixed on me as they were. I kissed her little hand. "I hope to come back very soon," I said to her and ran down the stairs as if I were being pursued. Maria tucked a bottle of cologne into my bag.

I found myself in an office in the Commando Piazza. I had shown my summons at the door, and they had escorted me inside. Italian officers were talking among themselves. The Italian colonel sat down at his desk and called the Greek interpreter. The others had withdrawn.

"You work at the Archbishop's headquarters?"

"Yes."

"A woman named Chartsa came to your office?"

"Yes."

"You gave her financial help and promised to give her money every month?"

"Yes. It isn't our business to look after beggars, but this woman lost her sons, and we want to help her survive."

"Do you know how she lost her sons?"

"No, I didn't ask. It is of no interest to us."

"Where did you get the money?" the Italian Colonel asked, eyeing me sharply, and the interpreter, after translating added impertinently, "Come on now, confess, it's well known that the Archbishop gets money from the Middle East."

Suddenly, I grasped the whole situation. I understood what they suspected us of. And this horrid little man, this traitor, with his puny stature, was trying to sink this one plank of rescue for our people.

I turned back to the Italian. "Colonel, do you perhaps speak French?"

"Certainly, if you prefer."

"Then let me explain to you directly what happens," I continued in French. "As you yourself know, our people are going through a frightful crisis of hunger and misery. All those who suffer from whatever reason take refuge at the Archbishop's headquarters. He tries to relieve and help those who are in want. He needs money. He started the Pan-Hellenic Fund, as you know. The Greeks consider it a mutual obligation for each to give according to his ability. Some more, some less. I'm sure you are a Catholic, Colonel. I'm sure you believe that in similar circumstances the Pope would do the same, and that the faithful would respond generously to his appeal."

60

The Colonel listened to me without interrupting, then stood erect.

"*Beneficenza, beneficenza,*" he turned and said to the interpreter.

The man had become so small that I could hardly see him.

They told me I could go. I went out by the main door. By the door through which free men pass. At the four corners of the street, friends and relatives were waiting for me.

I went home to my children. I looked at them, I touched them, as if I saw them for the first time. It was so wonderful that they were again my own.

"After pain . . . pleasure seems to follow." (*Phaedo* 60.c)

Poor Socrates! What utter renunciation of self he underwent in order to know pleasure!

10 May 1943

The office was full of hopeless people. Women who wailed, women who wept silently, and men who stood speechless like statues. This morning there were executions.

One father took me by the hand and confided to me, incoherently, but with a strangely sweet expression. "I used to hide behind the sheep-fold, and I was proud to see him go off in the morning to his work. He had a fine soft overcoat, beige, slit up the back, and he had yellow gloves like a real gentleman. But like a real gentleman, I tell you. At the Telephone Office they all loved him. I used to stroke that overcoat when he wasn't wearing it."

A very beautiful little girl wept inconsolably for her brother. They had executed him with Danielidis.

It was all I could do to keep myself erect. I felt that I was drowning in boundless grief. There were so many of them. I would have to speak words to these poor souls, trembling with love and maddened by man's cruelty. But words seemed so narrow, so limited, that I was ashamed to utter them. I sent to the Archbishop my fervent request that he himself would receive and speak to them.

They came into his office, fell on their knees, kissed his habit.

I don't remember what he said to them. Something about laying the foundations of a free fatherland. I remember better the picture; the girl at his feet, sobbing and weeping, and little by little getting to her feet, drying her eyes, and saying: "What does death matter . . . so long as Greece lives?"

20 May 1943

We have no time to catch our breath. Today they executed Andronikos. In the British army, he and Roussos had learned well how to use the transmitter. They came back to Greece in 1941 and with Danielidis sent regular information to the Middle East Command.

At a house in New Smyrna[11] while the transmitter was actually working, with the three wireless operators around it, the Nazis burst in. Roussos drew his pistol and killed the first German as he advanced. But a second officer shot Roussos instantly, and he fell dead. Danielidis continued to broadcast. His last words were: "The Germans are surrounding us. Long live Greece!"

2 June 1943

They have arrested the lawyer Costas Bouras. He was among the first to be informed of the murder of Tsigantes. Because he was a trusted and close collaborator and he also had to get rid of papers which would give away names of our people.

Since then, he was always with his radio and was the link between Psarros and the Middle East. Well informed on the Greek resistance, he has been sending fighters to Psarros' regiment.

The Germans suspect that Bouras knows many things. They are trying to break his nerve so as to find out. The interrogations which they put him through are torture.

Through the Archepiscopate and EKKA, we have connections with the jails, and we follow in agony all that happens there.

[11] Suburb of Athens.

13 June 1943

They continue to torture Bouras. They put an iron band on his head, and then squeeze it to try to make him confess. He shut his mouth tightly but fell senseless.

Each time after a difficult inquisition, the message comes to us: "Bouras did not speak." And something more. He sends us word as to what precautions we should take and which of our movements arouse the Nazis' suspicions.

Day and night they keep him in bonds. Day and night in a damp, sunless cell. The only interruptions are the frightful hours of the interrogations. Never for a moment does he give evidence of losing his courage, his spirit. Proud that he is able to hold out and not betray anyone, he lives with the faith that he is dying for a great Greece. And this faith gives him a superhuman strength. For consolation, alone there in jail, he hums softly a song of his own composition:

> At Samartzi's they took me—
> I know they're going to kill me
> For my dear fatherland.

18 June 1943

My spirit is heavy and oppressed. Nowhere can I find even a little peace. As if we are surrounded by countless mysterious loopholes, while shots are heard, far off, beside us, above us. Every moment is a fear—or an end.

This afternoon I went to the office. I was waiting for the sister of Goutis.[12] The secretary was pale and stammered softly:

"They are asking us for four priests for the prison."

I was terrified. "But how many do they intend to kill if they ask for so many priests?" I asked, trying to contain my anguish.

Goutis' sister arrived. She was hoping for some good news.

---

[12] André Goutis, petty officer in the Navy, under arrest. He was executed on 19 June 1943.

Poor soul, she was in agony. I said nothing to her. I suspected the worst, but I actually knew nothing.

I stayed a long time at the office and waited. It was late when we finally learned the names of those condemned to die. One finer than another—naval officers, wireless operators, brave young men who were holding the internal front of our nation.

To all of them they have offered pardon if they will give evidence, even at the last moment. Surely in vain. None of them will accept such a pardon.

19 June 1943

I got up at dawn. It was impossible to stay in bed. I put on something warm and sat out on the little terrace. I watched with wonder as the day advanced. The sun which gives us all warmth and heat—the sun which they will never see again.

20 June 1943

The priest who stood by the patriots through their last moments brought his report and, weeping, left it with us. His eyes, dazzled by the spectacle of those heroic deaths, still reflected the scene. For Bouras he wrote down the quatrain by Androutsos:

> His shoulders are a wall,
> His head a fortress,
> And his hairy chest
> Grass-grown ramparts.

21 June 1943

Dr. Christos Karvounis is in jail at Tripolis. A man came from Sparta and brought us the news. The Italians arrested him on the 12th of last month. Karvounis had received instructions from the Middle East to watch for a British officer. The Englishman, dropping by parachute, broke his leg. Naturally the doctor took him in and treated him. Some one must have betrayed them, and they were both arrested. By the same man who brought the information, I sent Karvounis books and the message that we will ask the Archbishop to try to get him out as quickly as possible.

28 June 1943

From prison Karvounis sends us word about certain persons who are playing a double game.

The Archbishop has taken steps with the Italians. He told them that a doctor has the duty to treat the injured, friend or foe, even when he doesn't know which he is. The Archbishop hopes that they will let Karvounis go free.

2 July 1943

This evening George Kartalis and Apostolos Kapsalopoulos came to see us. It has been a long time since I saw Kartalis. He was in a hurry and preoccupied. He is very worried about Psarros' regiment.

One night in May, the ELAS suddenly surrounded the 5/42 Evzones, and arrested their officers. The British saw to it that they were soon released. Afterward they urgently requested Psarros to regroup.

On June 23 a new attack by the ELAS.

The regiment suddenly found itself on the defensive and was forced to confront and repel the attack. Tragic days. To see brothers from the same house fighting each other in opposing camps, while foreigners exploit the country.

Although Colonel Psarros won, in order to avoid greater bloodshed he ordered his men to cease fire and to withdraw to Vounichora. He was deeply embittered. He didn't want to believe either in the indifference of the British or in the treachery of the Greek Communists. His disappointment was such that he decided to disband the regiment. All of Roumeli is mourning. Psarros was its security and its hope. His officers are hiding in the mountains. Both the Germans and the men of the ELAS are hunting them.

Kartalis gave me to understand that later, probably around August, he would make a flying trip to Egypt. "Do you want to send something to George Seferis"[13] he asked. I didn't answer. I wondered—would I see him again?—and my heart ached.

Who knows what George is suffering in Egypt? He who, wherever he is, so needs his own free soil. And he must have time for pure creativity, for rest. But here in the midst of this horror, I feel as if I were in Dante's Hell, pursued by madness! How I wish I could see George! He always helped to strengthen my spirit.

14 July 1943

A burning night. The house all dark so that we may have the windows open. Only Costakis, in spite of the heat, closes up his room. He must read. The children are sleeping on the small terrace. I stand at my window waiting for the little breeze which never comes.

Slowly, slowly I give myself over to the darkness, to the magic of the starry sky. Time passes. The night, the deep mystery deepens. I am alone on the whole earth. All the stars come to me, they are mine.

Somewhere far off there is an absurd war.

Here there is impenetrable beauty. A presence which I constantly seek is here beside me.

Thou knowest well, Lord God, that in this boundless love which tonight embraces Thee, there is my own love, too. And Thou givest Thy presence, Beloved; I feel it and I tremble.

[13] George Seferis, my older brother, diplomat, poet, Nobel Prize 1963.

20 July 1943

Psarros and Kartalis started for Pertouli.[14] They receive repeated messages from the Middle East Command to meet there with the British officers.

2 August 1943

Late this evening Apostolos passed by. The news of the Regiment 5/42 is good.

Kartalis and Psarros reached Pertouli on the 27th of July. The British received them and promised every assistance. Psarros, before reorganizing his troops, asked if the ELAS was in agreement. Kartalis saw the ELAS leaders again and said to them frankly: "We have plans for fighting the invader, not for fighting a civil war. If you intend to attack us, better tell us now."

All agreed that it was necessary for Psarros to reorganize, and they signed the agreement on July 31. The chief of EKKA was recognized as the military commander of Roumeli.

10 August 1943

Psarros is fortunate in all his officers. And Stephen Doukas has now gone to join him. Doukas is a truly humane man, but he is also a soldier. For him, duty in its highest form is a religion. Fatigue, deprivation, sacrifice, even his family, do not count as against duty.

Certainly many Greek officers are like that. But I have followed Doukas very closely, and in him I have had the good fortune to see these hard virtues developed to their highest degree.

[14] Village in Thessaly, seat of the General Command of the Resistance and of representatives of the Middle East Command.

15 August 1943

Today Apostolos said to Costakis, "What is to become of Psarros' officers? Their families are suffering a great deal. Can you speak to the Archbishop? Psarros comes to Athens. Perhaps it would be a good thing for the two of them to meet."

"I'll try," my husband answered.

21 August 1943

The Archbishop settled with Costakis the day and hour when he would receive Psarros at his house in Psychiko. They had a leisurely talk. The Archbishop gave him the money he needed and promised to give him more.

In these first days of the reorganization of the Regiment, such difficult days, this aid is precious.

22 August 1943

Apostolos came to our house again. He took out of his pocket two pieces of cigarette paper, fastened together with a pin. Typewritten in a column were the names of Psarros' officers. Beside each, the address of his house, and the sum of money which should be given to his family.

He left the money on the table and begged me to distribute it as quickly as possible.

When he left, I telephoned to Maria, my closest colleague.

She is a great help. Very quiet, courageous, intelligent, responsible, she has an inner compulsion to carry out perfectly any work she undertakes. We had agreed in advance about this distribution.

25 August 1943

At twilight, I took the papers and the money and started for Maria's house near Kolonaki Square.

9 December 1941. "The Italians have arrested Katina Doussi.
There is nothing about her to suggest that she is important."

14 September 1941. "I sit on the small veranda near the dining-room, hoping to cool off a little."

17 December 1943. "But what hell did the Nazis contrive in revenge?"

17 December 1943. "On the 13th of December the Germans encircled Kalavrita and began to ring all the churchbells madly."

12 February 1944. "In the evening hours of February 1, the Germans entered Amphissa."

12 February 1944. "The mountain ambulance of the regiment took refuge in the village of Karoutes." (Mountain pass between Amphissa and Karoutes.)

10 June 1944. "The Nazis turned to Distomo . . . made it their work to leave no living soul."

10 June 1944. "A great disaster yesterday at Distomo."

12 October 1944. "But I hurry on to the Archbishopric."

I went down Amalias Boulevard. I turned at the flower stands, and went forward along Queen Sophia Boulevard. A few people hurried by me on foot. A fine August rain was falling.

Suddenly my blood froze in my veins. Behind me, very near, I heard army boots following my steps. As I turned my head slightly, I saw a German officer looking at me insistently. Some one has betrayed me, I thought to myself.

What would happen? All those names, written down with their addresses, took on enormous, shining dimensions, and filled earth and heaven. For each one of them, arrest and interrogation. My heart was beating as if to break. Ahead I saw mass executions. I heard the all-too-familiar dirges of hopeless women. The end of the world opened up before me like an abyss.

I must do something quickly. I must somehow, as fast as possible, crumple up the cigarette paper like a handkerchief, get it into my mouth, chew it up, and swallow it. But the pin? How could I get rid of the pin which held the two pieces together?

"Shame on you!" I thought, "To stop at a pin. Swallow it, suffer, die. This affects only you. Of what importance are you, when you hold in your hands the lives of so many human beings?"

I hastened my step, but so did he. He was gaining on me.

"There's no time to lose. He is about to arrest me," I thought again.

I imagined his hand on my shoulder. Without further delay, I opened my handbag as though looking for my handkerchief and at the same time crumpled the cigarette papers into a ball. I coughed a little and put the wad into my mouth, along with the pin. Then I put the handkerchief back into the handbag.

It was the last moment, because now the Nazi was beside me. "Panayia," I implored, "make the paper dissolve, make the names disappear," and I tried to chew it up. The pin pricked my tongue, my gums. I couldn't swallow.

Now the Nazi was speaking. I did not understand what he was saying. In the evening air, I felt his foul breath. The pin continued to prick me. Suddenly, in the middle of what he was muttering, I made out two German words which I knew: "Strumpfe... Hotel." There was a flash of hope. Maybe this was just an ordinary male, a man who wanted a woman, and was offering her stockings?

We had reached the corner of Herodus Atticus and the Royal Garden. The second door is that of the German Embassy. And above the Embassy, on the third floor, is the home of my old friend, George Theotokas. Light breaks. "If it's a matter of arresting me, he will follow me in. Otherwise he will be ashamed because of his Embassy and will go away." I pushed the door open and went in.

I climbed the first steps as far as the elevator. There I stopped short. He was not following me. I continued to go up softly on foot. I stopped again and listened. Not a sound. I had already passed the turn in the staircase and no one had seen me. I took the paper, a formless mass, out of my mouth, drew out the pin, and threw it away. I caught my breath briefly and continued to climb. Every so often I pricked up my ears to listen. Absolute silence.

I reached George's floor. Beside his door there was an iron umbrella stand with earth in the bottom. I still held in my fist the formless wad of wet paper. I tore it into a thousand tiny pieces, dug up the earth, and buried them there. The silence all round continued unbroken.

I sat down on the top step. My legs would no longer hold me. "Whoever sees me here, it doesn't matter," I thought, and took a few deep breaths.

Suddenly the whole world was mine.

Such joy, such relief I had never known before. As if I had no body. If I had died at that moment, I would have flown like a happy bird straight into the sun. An utterly new freedom from care filled my being. Let them arrest me, let them hang me, what difference does it make!

I went out again into the street. Deserted. Here and there a few of our own people, weak poorly dressed. How much I loved them all! Whistling a dance tune, I found myself fairly flying home.

That same evening, I telephoned Apostolos to bring me a new list.

24 August 1943

We divided the work, Maria, John,[15] and I; by midafternoon we had finished the distribution. I'm worn out, but happy.

25 August 1943

Some of our men set fire to the tram station at Kallithea.[16] There is great damage. Hard days, boiling with excitement and suspicion.

26 August 1943

The communiqué from General Speidel says: "If in four days the perpetrators are not found, fifty hostages will be shot." Terrible hours. All those who have relatives in jail gather at the Archbishop's office. Their despair pours out with a dull roar from the walls, the windows, the doors. It chokes us too.

29 August 1943

The whole lower corridor of the Archbishopric and the lower steps are flooded with people. They are beside themselves. They demand that those responsible for the fire at Kallithea come forward. They speak against them. The agony they feel for their people in jail makes them unreasonable. The Bishop is not here. His secretary begs me to quiet them. Something must be done.

I remember that moment, when, in a fog, I went down two or three steps and heard myself as if I were not myself speaking to the people who had congregated: "We are all about to die. . . . Tomorrow, in a few moments, who among us will be alive? Let us not judge the other man. He may be a hero, he may be already

[15] John Pesmazoglou, professor of economics at the University of Athens.
[16] Suburb of Athens.

71

dead. What is left for us? A little kindness, a little love. Let us try, before we die, to reach out and touch these unique gifts of God."

I must have been persuasive, for they were silent, and slowly, slowly they dispersed.

31 August 1943

The Archbishop makes every effort, takes every possible step, to avert the reprisal. He sees Neubacher; he argues with him: he begs him to intercede. He sends a vigorous appeal to General Speidel. From morning to night he is seeing people. Both yesterday and today.

The decision to execute the hostages has not been republished.

1 September 1943

A communiqué from General Speidel announces that they have found certain persons suspected of the fire at Kallithea and the hostages will not be executed.

6 September 1943

The thankfulness of the people overflows. They crowd the Archbishop's headquarters from early morning. When the Bishop entered, they all fell to their knees.

7 September 1943

God help us! How careful one must be! Four Rural Police, sentries at the Kallithea jail, lost their lives because they were credulous.

Some individuals asked their help. They wanted, so they said, to acquire false identity cards and to join the resistance. These Rural Police took the photographs of the two traitors and promised to help them. With these photographs as evidence of guilt, the Nazis executed the policemen.

The truth is that many Rural Police have disappeared suddenly. They have obtained false identity cards, put on mufti, and gone to join Zervas or the 5/42 Regiment of Psarros. It was natural for the Germans to suspect them.

8 September 1943

A secret piece of news, an incredible piece of news, is in circulation. At first one man said it to another in confidence. But today it rings like a paean throughout the land: "The Italians have surrendered."

This morning for a short while triumph flooded our souls. This victory is ours too. Out of a curious desire to participate in an historic moment, I took my children and went to stand outside the Commando Piazza. No Italian flag, no carabinieri at the door. Ordinary people were coming and going. Torn papers overflowed the building and poured into the street.

What has become of the fortress which sat in judgment on the destinies and the lives of men? All this lie is scattered to the wind.

"The thunderbolt rules the universe." (Heraclitus)

9 September 1943

The Archbishop wants the Italians to free their prisoners. But who among them will dare so courageous an act? Everywhere panic and agony. No one takes the responsibility of helping us. The Italian plenipotentiary is in Rome.

Sunday evening. This day is not just twenty-four hours: it is a whole century. Thousands of things have happened. Last night the Archbishop saw the Italian director of prisons. The man agreed to open the prisons at a certain hour. But he disappeared.

At Kallithea the prisoners themselves broke down the doors and came out. The people received them with cries of joy. But the Nazis arrived, began to shoot at the crowd, and locked the jails again.

Macaskey[17] fortunately succeeded in escaping and taking refuge in a foreign Embassy.

The Germans were searching for him relentlessly, and suspected this particular embassy. Then the Archbishop was asked to undertake his custody.

Last night, with utmost precaution and with intervening stages, the Bishop took Macaskey to his home in Psychico.

Today, Sunday morning at ten o'clock, the telephone rang. It was the Archbishop.

"Something is going on at my headquarters," he said softly, "and I can't make out what it is. They got me on the telephone, I heard a frightened voice stammer something, and then we were cut off."

"I will go and see, Your Grace, and will let you know," I answered.

In five minutes I was in Philothei Street where the Archbishop's offices are located. The place was full of Germans. I went ahead, supposedly unconcerned, as if everything around me were normal. Some Germans were stationed at the door. I went in. Nobody tried to stop me or speak to me.

The building was empty. Everywhere there was indescribable disorder. Endless papers on the floor. All the drawers of the desks pulled out. Chairs and tables upside down. Even the busts of former archbishops overturned.

Suddenly I heard a small voice. I turned abruptly. It was Maria,

---

[17] Frank Macaskey, an English officer, correspondent of the *Times*, condemned to death by the Italians.

the cleaning woman, white as a sheet, and her voice came with effort.

"Maria," I said. "Where is the secretary?"

"The Germans took him," she answered, trembling.

"Where is Mitsos, the office boy?"

"The Germans took him," she said again, automatically.

"Never mind," I answered. "Don't be afraid. They haven't done anything. They will let them go."

I went up to the second floor. The disorder was even more striking. Nothing had remained in its place.

In our office the red and green cards had been scattered to the four corners and gave a slightly futuristic color to this storm-struck confusion.

I telephoned to Psychiko. "Your Grace, I am calling from the secretary's office. The Archbishopric is an occupied and ravaged fortress. They have searched the place as if they were looking for a needle."

I realized that this is what he expected to hear. He had been afraid that they would look for Macaskey there and had sent him to the home of Themistocles Tsatsos, my husband's brother, who lived nearby.

"I shall protest," he answered.

The Archbishop protested vigorously. But his protest cost him a further crisis.

This afternoon, while he was talking quietly in his home with Macaskey, his servant flung open the door of his office and shouted, "The Germans!"

He just managed to get the Englishman into the next room.

Four German officers of superior rank entered.

He received them with poise and politeness.

They came to ask official pardon for the morning search and went away immediately.

When, from the wide window, he saw their car disappear into the boulevard, he dropped with utmost relief into an armchair. Macaskey came in and they went on with their conversation about the resistance groups and about the advisability of Psarros bringing his regiment to Mount Parnis.

In the evening we went out to Psychiko to the houses of both the Archbishop and Themistocles Tsatsos. We met Macaskey.

Cultivated, well-mannered, he reminds one of Lord Byron. He loves Greece as if it were his own country. There we found out about General Speidel's suspicions. The Germans believed that the Archbishop had purchased the weapons of the Italians. Obviously it was weapons they were looking for this morning.

13 September 1943

The director of the Security Police came to an understanding with the Archbishop and himself accompanied Macaskey to the caique which will take him to the Near East.

14 September 1943

Finally some good news. Christos Karvounis was freed yesterday.

When something good happens, it always gives us the illusion of safety. But, in its game with man, Fate has an unbridled imagination which takes by surprise even those who are best prepared.

25 September 1943

How can the Germans so treat the Italians, their old allies? It is painful to see a human being mistreated, whoever he may be.

As for the true Greeks, their ancient humane tradition governs their conduct. They have forgotten the humiliations they suffered from the Italians; they have opened their houses to them, they have hidden them, they have looked after them. Now the Germans are the common enemy, the only enemy.

3 October 1943

A great disaster: Nikos Adam and Theophilou are arrested. We are all heart-broken. They have given incalculable services to the struggle. From June 1943 they constituted the sabotage corps of the secret organization APOLLO.

Nikos Adam is a simple fisherman. But what a hero! For him the most difficult things become simple. Last year at this time he transported officers from Turkey. Later he met Alexi[18] who entrusted him with materials, incendiary bombs, dynamite, underwater grenades, and assigned him to the sabotage of shipping.

Adam and Theophilou, an inspired junior officer in the navy, found heroic and intelligent companions and began the endless and astonishing chain of explosions. The *Conte de Savoia* sank at Piraeus. The German tanker burned like a Roman candle at Perama.[19] Later the *Manilla* at Keratsini,[20] and others—still others.

One by one the enemy boats burn up, and nobody understands, but nobody says a word.

APOLLO receives orders from Cairo to blow up the Bulgarian ship *Santa Fe*. Naturally the task is assigned to Adam's group. Theophilou takes charge. But he needs the help of a sailor on the *Santa Fe*. He looks around and finds Costas Kapoussidis, a good boy, eager, but inexperienced. He agrees to help and places the bomb which Theophilou gives him in the boiler room of the ship. The stoker sees him, and Costas loses his head. He confesses everything to the stoker.

"You're a Greek too. Don't give me away," he begs.

But the stoker was frightened and informed on him.

They seized Costas, Adam, Theophilou, and two others.

9 October 1943

Tragic day. They executed the Adam group. Adam took all the responsibility on himself, as if he were the only leader. The

[18] Liaison officer with the Allied Command.
[19] Port near Piraeus.
[20] Port near Piraeus.

others confessed with pride that they were the ones who fastened the explosive materials to the boats.

20 October 1943

Theophilou's wife came again today to the office. She too has great courage. She helped her husband with her whole soul. She would hide the torpedos in her house and convey them to the boat under her skirts. After her husband's arrest, during the interrogation, the Germans tried to frighten her. Her stout heart resisted every pressure, but now that he is gone, and she is alone with their four little ones to bring up, she is in despair.

"They had promised us that, if anything happened, we would lack nothing", she whispered with tears in her eyes.

We gave her what we had at our disposal that day.

25 October 1943

The Archbishop called me and said. "The organization APOLLO has turned over to me twenty million drachmas for monthly distribution to the families of the Piraeus saboteurs."

"And they are certainly expecting it, Your Grace!" I answered quietly, and then went on: "Do you think it would be too risky if we distribute this money now so that they can buy oil and food immediately? Who knows what value the money will have next month?"

The Archbishop laughed. "Agreed," he said. "I was sure that was what we would come to."

And that is what happened. We distributed the money on the spot.[21]

---

[21] Months passed. There was no other help available to these people. Theophilou's wife fell ill with an acute appendicitis. We took her immediately to the hospital. I saw her regularly. She herself had to buy the ice she needed. We did everything which it was possible to do to help her. But the poor woman died, in torment at abandoning her children.

2 November 1943

How many times they came to us and accused Kairis of working with the Germans! How many times they called him traitor!
I was choked with indignation and chagrin at the injustice, but my
duty was secrecy. In the universal struggle against the invader,
the most difficult lot had fallen to him. The contempt of the
Greeks and the danger that he would have to die for them. He
worked in the German service of fortifications in Southern
Greece, gathered the most valuable military and naval information, and, by means of his organization, transmitted it to the
Allies. The secrets which got out were important and the damage
to the enemy very great. They suspected him, they arrested him,
they sentenced him for espionage, and this morning they shot
him. His last words were spare and substantial, like his deeds.

"I will confront death like a man, with a quiet conscience, because I carried out my duty as a Greek patriot."

6 November 1943

At last the news from Roumeli justifies those of us who put our
faith in Psarros. The regiment of 5/42 Evzones was reconstituted
and was well organized. Second in command is Lieutenant Colonel
Laggouranis. His officers, brave patriots. They have arms from
the British.

All of September and October the regiment has been fighting the Germans under staff plans and discipline, like a regular
army unit. The battles it fights are heoric and victorious. At
various villages in Roumeli, the Germans suffer great losses in
both men and war materials and are fleeing in defeat.

Our officers and men outdo each other in patriotism, perform-
ing deeds of utmost self-sacrifice. Psarros is well pleased.

12 November 1943

Somewhat delayed, there came to us the wonderful news that
Amphissa is liberated. The fighters of the 5/42 Regiment marched

triumphantly into the town. The people were beside themselves with joy and regard the 5/42 Evzones as liberators. The women are caring for them. They have set up hospitals to treat the wounded and sick.

18 November 1943

Today Apostolos recounted to us a characteristic episode which demonstrates Psarros' concern for the civilian population. Captain Dedoussis, daring as always, with his company attacked a a German truck full of soldiers. All the Germans were killed and the truck was burned. Immediately Psarros ordered three companies to surround the village and guard them. The villagers should under no circumstances suffer a reprisal. And no reprisal took place.

19 November 1943

On the 7th of November, the Germans abandoned Lidoriki. Roumeli is free at last.

21 November 1943

Apostolos passed by our house and gave me an address in Pankrati.[22]

"Kartalis is coming from the mountains tomorrow," he said. "About nine in the evening he will be at Samartzi's cafe. Can you meet him there and take him to this address? He has no idea where he is to spend the night."

I asked some further information and promised to go.

[22] Section of Athens.

I covered my head with a peasant kerchief, and at nine I was at the cafe, alongside the theatre.

Lots of people were coming and going. All unshaven, dirty, uncouth. In a moment I spotted George Kartalis with a rather rough-looking man. He was wearing his old army coat, and was unshaven, white with dust. I went near and greeted him. "Good evening, George."

"My sister," he said abruptly, as, with a worried air, he introduced me to the man.

I waited while they finished their conversation and then we left.

In silence we took a taxi, left it at Syntagma Square, and took another. When we came near the house the address of which I had been given, we left that taxi too and continued on foot. He was worn out. He told me he would pass by our house tomorrow. I said goodby, and when they opened the door to him, I started back on foot.

I went ahead in the darkness. I was comforted by the hope that a taxi would appear. But nothing. Absolutely deserted. Here and there I turned on my flashlight to get my bearings. Suddenly, on Olga Boulevard, shooting broke out from the two sidewalks, as if there were thousands of men in opposing armies. Where were they all hidden, these men from whom not even a breath was heard? And what were the Germans doing?

"Don't turn on your flashlight or they'll get you," some one nearby said to me.

I went on through the thick darkness. The surface of the street was uneven. I would fall and get up again. I tried to go as fast as I could so as to escape from this battle, this Hell.

I arrived home past ten o'clock, worn out, bleeding, my stockings in rags, my clothes muddy. My husband was worried about me. He knew that they regularly make arrests at Samartzi's and that I was going there.

"I fell right into a battle on Olga Boulevard," I told him.

But the agony is forgotten when we are all together again.

This evening Kartalis came to the house. We had not spoken much in the taxi—just enough to appear natural. But there was a great deal to talk about. He has come from Egypt, and also from the mountains. At last I could ask him about George Seferis. Since yesterday I have been longing to hear. He saw a lot of George in Cairo, and he is well.

"George is tormented with homesickness, and his anxiety for the country leaves him no peace," he went on. "When the two of us sat alone together, over and over his distress was apparent."

All of us are paying for this war, I thought—each one where God has placed him.

Afterward Kartalis talked about Psarros.

"We've gone around through many villages together," he said. "We've slept in the same room, with the fireplace between us to try to keep warm because the snows have begun. We have talked for hours about a free country. Plans and dreams. Neither he nor any of his men has ever deprived a villager of anything. The people up there worship Psarros and his soldiers. One of his officers is better than another. Since August 16, Doukas has been with him. Psarros sent him to the Roumeli command at Karpenissi with Major Vlachos.[23] It is a difficult job."

Kartalis was transformed as he spoke. This skeptic, ready to mock almost everything, perhaps in order to fight his innate romanticism, was all emotion and concern for his responsibilities.

He frowned when he spoke of the lack of understanding among the various groups.

"In the Middle East, with all our good intentions, we did not reach agreement. Here everything is still more difficult. The ELAS does not obey the orders from the British headquarters."

There was a long silence. Then he went on again, changing the subject.

"There is something else we must think about seriously. We

---

[23] Psarros thought that it would be wiser that EKKA Headquarters of Roumeli be at Karpenissi, near the British Liaison Officer and close to the ELAS Headquarters. He placed two of his best officers there: Major Vlachos and Captain Stephen Doukas.

need help. Up there the snow falls all the time. The men are living in freezing cold. We need blankets, sweaters, anything woolen. Could you help us? You must understand the double significance of such help. Every piece of clothing will keep someone warm, and also it will remind him that Athens is with him."

24 November 1943

Last night I didn't close my eyes. I was searching for a quick solution. If I could in a few days prepare a first installment of woolens, what joy it would bring to those heroic men! But someone must help. How can I bring off such a job by myself?

This morning I looked up some of my friends who work in organizations. Without giving myself away, I sounded out each one's courage and learned what each one had at her disposal.

All those who had the capacity to help were very guarded. Those who were venturesome had no capacity. Then I thought of Lena Zarifi. Lena has determination and moral courage. She has a responsible position in many organizations. I have spoken to her about EKKA. She agrees that Psarros' regiment is a serious resistance movement and above reproach. She had met Kartalis and Kapsalopoulos at our house. When young Lenos, her son, asked to be used in the resistance, we thought about the matter together and put him in touch with EKKA. So it came about that Lenos Zarifis, while still in the gymnasium, worked in the secret information service of EKKA.

25 November 1943

I saw Lena Zarifi again. We talked frankly and confidentially about the needs of the Regiment, and I explained to her what I had been thinking.

"You are at the head of a service as I am," I said to her. "You will charge to my service a given number of sweaters which you will not send to us. Instead, Psarros' men will get them up to the mountains. But I wouldn't for a moment want to deprive the families of the executed, not in the slightest degree. I have taken full responsibility for them. I will ask you to make it easy for them to take what they need directly from the Red Cross."

Lena accepted the plan enthusiastically.

26 November 1943

It is a great thing when something you have imagined really comes about, and at once. Lena sent me eighty pullovers. The same evening Kartalis, amazed at finding them ready, picked them up and sent them off to Amphissa. Not even he could believe that it was so quickly accomplished.

27 November 1943

All night torrential rain. I couldn't sleep. But this morning I opened the window on the most brilliant winter day. The earth was washed clean. The sun, bright and warm, like August. The telephone rang. I took up the receiver and heard the news. "Yesterday at Sparta at Monodendri, the Nazis shot one hundred and seventeen, all the flower of the city, among them Christos Karvounis." I turned to stone. I didn't understand. I didn't want to understand. The man repeated the same words. I can still hear him. Yesterday morning at Monodendri, they shot one hundred and seventeen. The four sons of Tzivanopoulos and Dr. Karvounis. A dead man for every house. All Sparta is lamenting. If the whole town had burned to the ground, the evil would have been less.

"But why?" I managed to ask.

"They killed a German soldier at Monodendri." The man at the end of the line said it to me again.

I went to my office for the daily tasks. Like an automaton, I listened to the peoples' problems. In the morning, and now in the evening still, one thought is always there in my mind, and it will not let me rest. "Christos Karvounis will not see Greece free." This great longing which made him move heaven and earth, which made him live and die every moment, has plunged into the chaos of the unfulfilled. I try to recall Monodendri. I have passed there going to Sparta. The hairpin turns had made me dizzy.

28 November 1943

Some one came from Sparta. I listened for hours while he talked about the death of the Man. Legends fill the air. But this is history. At the last moment, the Germans respected the distinguished scientist, and granted him pardon. Karvounis asked that this pardon be granted to one of the Tzivanopoulos brothers.[24] So that their mother should not weep for all four sons at once. The Germans refused. Then Karvounis rebelled.

"You are a barbarous people," he said to the officer in perfect German. "I am ashamed to have wasted eight years in your country. Eight years gone, lost."

The Nazi was furious. He reddened, and then with all his might he hit Karvounis on the arm with the butt of his pistol.

When they picked up the dead at Monodendri, Christos Karvounis had a broken arm.

6 December 1943

We have lots going on at home this evening. Lena Zarifi sends sweaters regularly. Psarros' men come by and take them.

I have become so accustomed to these missions that I was not afraid to explain them to my children. I need them. I have to have some secret help, and the servants must not suspect. Often little Dora waits at the outer door and keeps it open so that they will not have to ring the bell. George Kartalis and Stephen Doukas

[24] For a long time, Mrs. Tzivanopoulos made her son's beds every morning and turned them down every evening.

said goodby to us as they left to rejoin the Regiment. They went off pleased.

10 December 1943

All night endless shooting in Omonia. As darkness comes, battles break out in the middle of Athens and continue until morning.

12 December 1943

Many are unjustly killed. It seems that day before yesterday in the battle at Omonia a German noncommissioned officer was wounded. Today the Germans shot ten hostages.

17 December 1943

Like the chorus in an ancient tragedy, one after another, black-garbed women entered my office in an endless line. Their faces were like marble, motionless, with a uniform expression of death which I have never seen before. The first one spoke with effort.

"We come from Kalavrita.[25] We are not all. Most of us remained behind."

When we heard "Kalavrita," we shuddered. For four days now the air is full of horrible rumors, like those in the old days about Missolonghi. We live in horror of the sufferings inflicted on these people. We keep hearing—"Kalavrita is burning. Kalavrita is being butchered."

Now Mrs. Fefé, a great lady from Kalavrita, has recounted to us what happened, and the truth proves more savage than all the rumors.

"The Germans and the ELAS joined battle outside Kerpini. The ELAS killed the wounded prisoners." But what Hell did the Nazis contrive in revenge?

[25] Town in the Northern Peloponnesus.

On the 13th of December the Germans encircled Kalavrita and began to ring all the churchbells madly. The people came out into the streets. They were taken to the school courtyard. There the Germans separated the men and boys over fifteen and drove them beyond the cemetery to a hill above the town. Because from there the whole place was visible. Opposite them they placed two machine-guns so that no one should escape. Then they set fire to Kalavrita. The men saw their houses burning, and heard the shrieks of their people. They were maddened to desperation, believing that their women and children were burning too. The executioners, after sadistically enjoying their torment, turned the machine guns on them and killed them all.

They locked the women and children in the school-house and set fire to it. But it appears that an Austrian officer couldn't stand it, and being the last one to leave, he removed the guard and opened the doors.

The women poured out, choking with the smoke, and began to hunt for their husbands. The Germans had believed that they were leaving no living creature behind them and had gone away.

And Mrs. Fefé continued, "We found our husbands, our sons, our brothers. But how did we find them! Only God knows! And then we began their horrible burial, there in the frozen earth. We hadn't the strength to dig. We dug with our nails and fell fainting on the ground."

20 *December 1943*

Mrs. Fefé came back alone. A remarkable woman, she feels responsible for her whole town. She helps us greatly to help the others. She is the link between our office and the women of Kalavrita. All of them alone—all of them without hope.

21 *December 1943*

Today, among others, a woman came to my office. Sweet, gentle, she came close to me and spoke softly.

"My son is confined at Haidari. For days now I have been trying to see him and I cannot. His name is Deimezis. Do you perhaps know anything about him? Has something bad happened to him?"

The moment I heard the name I froze. I remembered it. I had seen it on the most recent list of slain hostages. "What is his Christian name?" I asked, to gain time.

"Alexander," she answered. "He is a petty officer in the Navy."

I hadn't the strength to speak the truth, nor could I lie to those blue eyes which looked at me with complete trust.

"Would you like to wait a little till the crowd goes away?" I whispered. "Then I can look at all the information I have"— and I had her sit down near me.

People came, people went. I spoke with them all, but my mind was fastened on the woman who sat there beside me. How to tell her? And what to tell her?

I looked again secretly at the lists in the hope that I had been mistaken. The name Alexander Deimezis appeared among the first hostages shot on December 16. Lord God, how could I tell her?

The moment came when we were left alone. She looked at me and waited patiently. I pretended to search for something in my file.

"They have taken him away from Haidari," I said. "I don't find him anywhere."

For a few moments we were silent. A spasm in her throat revealed her emotion. Then with difficulty she spoke.

"Perhaps they killed him."

I took her hand. I had a dreadful pain in my stomach, my head. How unbearable it all is! Her silence, and the downward curve of her lips, and her eyes which looked but did not see! But why doesn't she cry out like the others? Where is her spirit? Words are nothing in the face of this silence. I kept holding her hand. Time passed. Then very softly she spoke.

"It is half past three—time to go."

"Shall we go down together?" I asked shyly. And we stood up. We went out into the street. Not even the good sun of the winter afternoon, the warm, magical sun, could help us. It seemed like a false scenic effect and left us both frozen.

At home I sat down mechanically at the table. My husband and children had already eaten. They looked at me curiously. We had a turtle in the garden, and every morning we gave it a little grass. We all loved her. Some one, I think it was Eudoxia—said, "The turtle died."

Suddenly everything began to whirl around me. I got up, and with difficulty got to my room. I threw myself face down on the bed and broke into sobs. My children looked at me with amazement. I felt little Dora stroking me gently, and heard her saying to me, "Don't cry, mummy. I'll get you another turtle." I was shattered. I could no longer control my nerves.

22 December 1943

This morning in the office, among the innumerable faces, there was again her face. Why? I thought she would hate me.

"Let me sit down, let me come," she said to me.

And even when I go home, I see her eyes looking at me. I feel chaos opening under my feet.

Vanity of vanities! The poor human conscience a flash in the black darkness.

For a fleeting moment the ivy on the opposite wall catches my attention . . . this too a lie. Truth is self-deception. I don't want to see. . . . Darkness . . . shadows . . . . Lord God, why hast Thou forsaken me?

27 December 1943

These days I am not well.

1944

Lift up the light of Thy
countenance upon us.

Psalms 4:6

1 January 1944

Today, New Year's Day, a wave of real hope floods the house. Everything that is great and decisive starts from heaven to come to us. It passes and is lost; but the miracle—we feel it—will stand in our hearts.

"And next year—free!" we say to one another, and we believe it.

On my plate at the table I found a card from Despina and Dora. It is a picture of a boat with Greek flags on the open sea. And underneath: "We shall live, and we shall break out the flags."

14 January 1944

Our missions for Psarros' regiment are an unbroken struggle. But it is a labor which gives us great satisfaction. As if we too are fighting the enemy.

18 January 1944

From the mountains they ask us for more blankets. The winter is very severe. Somehow we must find them.

20 January 1944

I went to Lena Zarifi. "What can we do, Lena, about these blankets?" I said. "Yesterday again I had a message from up there. They are buried in snow. At the Archbishop's we haven't a single one. Everything we have we distribute immediately." She listened to me thoughtfully.

21 January 1944

Lena telephoned me yesterday afternoon. When it grew dark, she came with a trustworthy taxi driver and brought me sixty blankets. With astonishing mastery, she put them in sacks. I helped her all I could, but I didn't have her dexterity. The same evening the sacks left for Amphissa.

22 January 1944

The Germans suspect that the Allies will undertake a landing in Greece. They are concentrating their forces in the area of Gravia, Bralo, and Livadia. It appears that they want to retake Amphissa[1] and open the road to Naupactos. Colonel Psarros has agreed to defend that area. He must prevent the Germans from advancing. He has made his plans and organized his regiment for defensive action.

23 January 1944

The news that reaches us is meager and delayed. Poor Apostolos, who realizes our agony, comes every evening and tells us whatever he learns.

Psarros has placed his officers and his men at strategic points in Roumeli.[2] For twenty days, Captain Kaimaras and his company have been guarding the highest point of the road from Gravia to Amphissa. There are daily snowstorms and thick fog.

On the 11th of January, the first Germans appeared. Our men fell on them with such violence that they had to retreat. But in a short time they returned with their forces increased.

27 January 1944

Some one must have come from the mountains. That is why Apostolos was so well informed this evening. This indomitable

---

[1] Psarros had occupied Amphissa since 12 October 1943 with the 5/42 regiment of Evzones.
[2] Section of Greece south of Thessaly.

man, who wants always to stand above events, overflowed with joy and emotion as he spoke. The moment they saw the Germans, our officers with their automatics in their hands gave the signal for the attack. The men could not be held back. They rushed into battle shouting their war cry, 'aera!" The Germans retreated again with heavy losses both in dead and in war materials. Of our men, Sergeant Galiotis was killed. Badly wounded, his two legs cut off by a mine, he fought on, throwing hand grenades.

For the second time the Germans had tried to advance and had been turned back by the 5/42 Evzones.

The relief and enthusiasm in Roumeli are tremendous. Psarros is their adored hero.

12 February 1944

We follow with agony the movements of the Germans as they come back with very great forces and armored cars to the place where they were defeated.

From their new exploits we are coming to know Psarros' officers better. All of them, without exception, fight heroically, true Greeks.

But no heroism can withstand the torrent of the enemy army and its firepower.

In the evening hours of February 1, the Germans entered Amphissa.

The people locked themselves in their houses. Many fled to the surrounding villages. The mountain ambulance of the Regiment took refuge in the village of Karoutes. All the wounded were rescued.

20 February 1944

For a little while yesterday we were amused by the dangerous game of Thanasis Athanasiadis.

He had left Athens with Doukas and Kartalis, carrying documents for the forthcoming conferences of the resistance groups.

On the way, Doukas asked him, "Loaded down as you are, do you have your own identity card and travel permit in order?" Thanasis answered with spirit: "I have neither. I just didn't have time to get them ready."

"You must be mad," said Kartalis. "What will you do at the checkpoints?" Thanasis laughed, "Don't worry. You'll find out, and you'll laugh too."

At the first roadblock, he jumped out first and began to shout: "Identity cards and permits, quick, boys—identity cards and permits. Hurry up now, don't delay us!" And he set about gathering up the papers from the passengers, and presented them to the German. The man, stupified by the speed and efficiency of the job, followed after Thanasis, smiling and friendly. He seemed grateful for the help. And he didn't think to ask Thanasis for his own papers.

He played the same game at the other roadblocks, and the Germans reacted the same way.

His two friends followed the whole affair with palpitations, and when the last checkpoint was behind, they all had a hearty laugh.

9 March 1944

On the 15th of February at Myrophyllo[3] the resistance groups and the British military mission began discussions looking toward the unification of the struggle. As was to be expected, they came to nothing. The Communists who run the ELAS have their own plans.

As soon as the deliberations were over, Colonel Psarros had to leave. He was to start military action as soon as possible. In accordance with the Allied Operation "Ark," the 5/42 Regiment had many missions to carry out. As Psarros was leaving, he appointed as his representatives his two colleagues, Kartalis, and, for military matters, Doukas. Yesterday, after many adventures, the two of them arrived in Athens and gave us all the news.

[3] Village in Epirus.

15 March 1944

The most bitter experience of all is that of being no longer surprised by the senseless cruelty of man.

Utter solitude . . . neither people, nor friends. . . . . Exhausted from fatigue, the soul seeks no human contact. Fortunately, there is the night.

3 April 1944

This spring of 1944 lets the dawn of liberation peer through, but it seems to be the crucial point of our tragedy. On the one hand, the Nazis, maddened like the whip-wielding Ajax,[4] do not know where to strike and whom to kill. Everything escapes them, everything frightens them. On the other hand, the Communist party pursues its own objectives and pitilessly wipes out the Greeks, trying to bring about their complete collapse.

18 April 1944

The doorbell rang! Kartalis came into the house without speaking to anyone! He threw himself on Angelos' bed! He wept as a man weeps, with the complete honesty of his bitterness. No one spoke to him. He could not be comforted. Costakis and Angelos and I listened to him dumbfounded, without a word. Yesterday the ELAS guerillas killed Psarros and more than 150 of the officers and men of the 5/42 Regiment.

19 April 1944

Anguish chokes us. Every moment we wait to hear more.

[4] In the myth, Athena sent madness on Ajax. In his frenzy, he turned on the flocks of the army, slaughtered some beasts, and led others to his tent, believing them to be the Greek leaders on whom he wanted to take vengeance.

Doukas has returned to Athens. That is something.

He had gone with letters from EKKA for the British Colonel Chris, and for one of the ELAS leaders, Bakirtsis,—letters which begged them at all cost to prevent the collision. But he could not reach Klima because the ELAS guarded all the passes. He found himself alone with Kokorelis, brother of an officer in the 5/42 Regiment. They reached Aigion by boat. They looked for a ship to Monastiraki so as to meet Psarros. The ELAS guerrillas got wind of it and went after them. After endless hardships, yesterday they finally reached Patras on foot. There they found the remnants of the Regiment. There they learned of the murder of their leader. There Kokorelis saw his brother, severely wounded with a broken spine.

20 April 1944

Today I hurried to our chief of police. I asked him for false identity cards for the survivors of the 5/42 Regiment who had gone to Patras. I gave them to Doukas who had asked me for them. He took care to put them directly into the men's hands so that they may avoid new troubles with the Germans.

26 April 1944

Every day we hear descriptions of the catastrophe which befell Psarros and his men, and they are nightmares. Extreme sufferings, degradations. But why so much hate? Why all this evil? We keep watch and count the names of the men who have escaped. Profound relief for everyone found alive.

28 April 1944

Still burning with hope for a glorious liberation, we gather in the evening, and each one of us, soul in mourning, gives his information. Day by day the news is more horrible. All these courageous men, without self-interest, without political ideologies, simple soldiers that they were, butchered, unburied in the lanes of villages, and first of them all—Psarros.

The war will surely end, and the Allies will win. But what will become of Greece?

29 April 1944

The needs of the resistance gradually absorb the officers who survived. Kartalis is leaving for the Middle East, for Lebanon.

And so time begins to drizzle down on Psarros and his Regiment.

We fall to the bottom of the sunless precipice, and again we try tooth and nail to clamber to the light. To bring about the day of liberation which is in danger of becoming a day of lasting slavery.

30 April 1944

I cannot close my eyes. At night I walk about the house like a ghost. I am haunted by the idea of disaster, and I expect it at any moment. The time is endless. I am in my office at eight o'clock. The city and the countryside are seething.

The first of May, 1944

As I entered my office, I was taken by surprise. So early in the morning and so many people—why? The legal advisor to the Archbishop was there too.

"What's going on?" I asked.

"It's a good thing you came early," the secretary said. "The Archbishop wants to see you."

I presented myself in his office. He was livid.

"Listen," he said, "today at dawn they executed two hundred

hostages at Kaissariani.[5] They will not give out the names under any circumstances, not to me, not to the Red Cross, not even to the German Red Cross, as I begged them to do. They won't listen to anything. They have gone mad. They are afraid of their own shadows."

I went back to my office. My head was empty. Two hundred killed. How many women will again pass through this terrible hour! There is no help anywhere. All is finished.

Rebellion cried out in me. By what right do these miserable little human brains bring about such an inferno of pain?

A little strength, where can we find anymore just a little strength?

At nine they telephoned to us from the police station at Kaissariani. The Germans had sent the clothing of the victims there, and the police asked to take the things away as soon as possible. We sent a truck immediately, with a clerk from the office to take delivery of them. We had at our disposal a small storeroom on Apollo Street and gave instructions to have the things taken there.

When I entered that storeroom, my mind clouded over. All these jackets, the warmth of life still in them, limp sleeves reaching forward, full of secrets—they wanted something, were seeking something, and could no longer tell us.

I took one jacket in my hands. The edges were very worn. In the pocket a crumpled paper, a note: "If I do not manage to publish my book, you will find my manuscript. . . ." No name.

In another jacket: an identity card, just a name. In another, nothing, not even that. In still another, a note: "That Stelios talks to me as if he didn't know men at all. He seems to be a nice fellow, but gullible. . . . Mother came to see me; how her hand trembled. . . ." I closed the door and fled as if I were pursued.

In the office we all agreed that at first we would be alone in the storeroom so as to gather together whatever identity cards and notes we might find in the clothing. We would learn as many names as possible. Then we would open the doors to the people.

And so it happened. We worked all day. Not a breath was

5 Suburb of Athens.

heard. Involuntarily, toward evening, I turned and saw Maria. She was so pale, I was afraid she would faint. I took her by the hand and led her into the street. A fresh breeze struck us in the face.

"You've done enough for today, Maria. Go home," I said. She didn't at all want to leave, but I insisted. She was so young, almost a child, and she was beginning life with this horrible experience.

We picked out seventy-five names. In the clothing of the other one-hundred-twenty-five we found no sign of identity.

I went home at ten. Despina and Dora were asleep. My husband, whom the Nazis were also hunting, was sleeping at a friend's house.

"I'll get into a hot bath without seeing anyone," I thought with relief. I went along the corridor to the bathroom. But there on a chair was something which terrified me. I turned to ice. A suit of my husband's, with sleeves outstretched like those of the two hundred. My legs began to tremble. I sat down on the chair in the corner and looked at it distracted. I didn't dare go forward to touch it. In my fingers I still felt the touch of the dead men's clothing.

"Take the master's suit away," I said with difficulty to Eudoxia, who was looking at me as if I were mad.

"But I have to brush it," she said.

"Take it away, please, so that I won't see it again", I stammered in a choked voice.

Death, like a heavy and painful presence, stood behind me. I couldn't escape from its shadow. I was suffocating.

2 May 1944

We opened the doors of the storeroom to the public. An endless crowd came in. The whole of Apollo Street was overrun with women. Women from Athens, from Penteli, from Eleussis. At one moment it seemed to me that all the suffering women of Greece were there.

All those who recognized names went away with lamentations and dirges, taking with them the few belongings of their dead. But the others went in, rummaged among the things like mad women, and, when they found nothing, they started to go away. Then they weren't satisfied, so they came back and searched again. Some immediately found some piece of their man's clothing; others were tortured for hours.

One mother found her son's clothes, covered them with kisses, and suddenly fell senseless. Through her tears she had seen the jacket of a second son. Two children lost in the same hour—it is too much.

At the same moment we heard a low dirge, a chant, from one corner. The words and the rhythm were broken by sobs.

> *My child, alone I raised you*
> *My comfort, with my own hands I raised you,*
> *You were beautiful and pure like a girl—*
> *Don't go away, my child. Come back.*

The woman sat on the floor and clutched her son's jacket to her breast. And she went on singing her dirge in a rhythmic monotone.

And that dark girl with big eyes who took me by the sleeve and said, "I know they killed him, but I don't understand. I want to see him, alive or dead. I want to see him, himself."

The thought stabbed me—how vital is the need to bury one's own!

But another woman from Penteli made me sit down beside her on the threshold. Her eyes had the expression of an animal about to die. She clutched the clothing tightly and said to herself: "I am useless, finished. Whatever I had, whatever I was, vanished with him. Let me find a hidden spot, on the earth, where I can lie down and die alone, with no one near me."

The aged Simeon spoke to Panayia, and his words were written in flame: "A sword shall pierce through thy own soul also." (Luke 2:35)

The sword was there, planted in the woman's heart.

Hours and hours of frantic grief. We no longer knew whether we had our senses. Neither what we heard nor what we said had any meaning. Black despair spread out and darkened the day.

By evening the storeroom was empty. The wailing ceased. The infamous Nazis knew what they were doing when they withheld the names.

At home I made no effort to rejoin life. Death had come down to the earth, it was there with us, it was welcome. As if I had fought, hand to hand, with all the sorrows of earth, and now the ebbing tide was taking me out to sea into the light. Nothing touched me. "My peace I give unto you." (John 14:27) I thank Thee, my Lord.

Gently, gently all these horrible nightmares of life dissolved. The compassion, the fear for the future of loved ones, the humiliation of slavery, the anguish of partings. I was helpless, so helpless, in the blue light of the ocean, endlessly waiting.

And death had taken on the shape of love. Like nothingness, like a mystical change to another form, like a relentless pull toward infinity.

The whole meaning of life is love, I thought. And this thought cut me like a knife.

Lord God, make me not love, I don't want to love. Naked, alone, indifferent, free—toward Thee, for Thee.

But I am so exhausted. The mother from Penteli was right. . . . when the body is spent, we fall into sleep; when the body and soul are spent, let us fall into death. There is nothing evil about it. We parcel out our souls, and the end comes, the ebbing tide, the light.

I found Despo again. As if she came from far away. . . . Pale, eyes full of sorrow, she explained to me that nothing ends with death.

"Don't you feel that the boundaries disappear, and that we are all together? A little spreading of the soul, and the warmth of their love is near you."

This woman is a great help to me. In our office, haunted by all the loves and partings, she knows that among all the thousands each one is unique. She knows that love is the only understanding men have. And her word of comfort is her very soul.

5 May 1944

To my Death

Come to me, I am beautiful
My soul full of longing
From love's harsh service
My senses eager
Like the earth on fire.

Come to me, I am lonely
On the ascent to the Mystery
I left behind the unripe man
And my loneliness is heavier than life.

Come, worthy, handsome, strong,
Opening the heavy gate of Revelation
toward perfect love.
A woman, bound to my cross,
I spread my arms to You,
Wise, sure in love and sense,
And I lose myself in You —
You are my death, and You are all my life.

This is the hour,
And it is Yours, my Lord.
All words are ended,
And I hear the cry of truth
Start from the bowels of earth.

8 May 1944

They are watching the Archbishop's headquarters. And they are watching the house where he is staying, in Democritus Street.

15 May 1944

Yesterday the Nazis arrested the Archbishop. He is in bed, very ill, angina again. They did not move him. But they put guards outside his house, guards on the stairways of the apartment building. And the endless interrogations began, first by Bach, the chief of the S.D., and later by other officers. Interrogations about his contacts with the Middle East and with the resistance fighters, about his negotiations with Psarros, about his meeting with Tsigantes. Interrogations about how he finds the money to help the families of the slain.

19 May 1944

They have decided to take the Archbishop to Germany. This is a grave hour. No one believes he will come back alive.

"Your Grace, I shall go with you," one of our people said to him.

This offer, coming from the heart of a devoted friend, made the Archbishop happy.

20 May 1944

By good luck Neubacher has returned to Athens. Like the politician he is, he has better judgment. He sensed the great popular indignation that mistreatment of the Archbishop would provoke, and he telephoned to Berlin to cancel the removal to Germany.

29 May 1944

Day by day the Archbishop's health worsens. The heat is suffocating. The doctors are asking that he be permitted to stay in his house in Psychiko.

30 May 1944

They moved the Bishop to Psychiko under escort. He traveled in an automobile from the S.D.[6] There again the same surveillance, the same isolation.

2 June 1944

The detention of the Archbishop is a heavy blow to our services. The communications and the gifts are reduced to almost nothing. We try with great effort to find the money we need to continue the support of our needy families. Naturally those who are in trouble and in want always come to us. And they express their requests with touching restraint. There is nothing demanding about them. They ask about the Archbishop with anguished concern. During all these difficult years of slavery, they have continued to think of him as infallible. He has always pointed out to them the road to national honor and solidarity. He has saved thousands of men from starvation and death. And now he himself is in the hands of the hangman.

5 June 1944

In my little office goes on continuously the tragic monologue of the living about their dead. The air is redolent with freedom, as it is in spring with fragrance. And though the Greek refuses to accept death, it spreads and suffocates, and survival is a matter of chance. The enemy is unaccountable. Perhaps he wants vengeance because he is leaving our country without ever having been a real conqueror.

10 June 1944

A great disaster yesterday at Distomo.[7] The news keeps com-

---

[6] *Sicherheitsdienst* (Security Service), the police element of the S.S.
[7] Village in the nome of Boeotia.

ing. There outside the little town the ELAS collided with the Germans. The losses on both sides were minimal. But the Nazis turned to Distomo, and, rabid, made it their work to leave no living soul. Men, women, old people, children, and twenty babies in their cradles—they killed them all. Then they set fire to the town. As if it were necessary for their own survival that there should be only devastation around them.

12 June 1944

We haven't seen a single woman from Distomo at the Archbishopric. Whatever women there were are dead—they and their children.

13 June 1944

Time passes. We bury our heads in our daily tasks. We try to forget our responsibility as human beings in the face of these consummated crimes. So ignoble our slavery—so terrifying our impotence. If only we could set fire to their staff headquarters and burn ourselves up with them. Samson was a free man.

15 June 1944

On a nearby corner is an apartment building where a friend of ours lives. The concierge is a good man. He reports to us every day on the surveillance of our house. A man in gabardine is always there, watching my husband.

My husband sleeps away from home now, sometimes with one friend, sometimes with another.

Messages from the Middle East. They are asking him to go there.

We are in regular touch with "Homer."[8] He is director of the

---

[8] During the occupation, "Homer" was the pseudonym of Dionysios Verros, then Captain.

Second Bureau of investigation and organizes the departures for Egypt. This morning he sent word for Costakis to get ready to leave.

16 June 1944

My husband left.

18 June 1944

Two days have passed, heavy, oppressive. I have no news.

19 June 1944

I was in a cafe with Lena. Suddenly I saw passing by outside a Costakis who was unshaven, his clothes all wrinkles, a knapsack on his back. He was going toward Philellinon Street, and he seemed to be looking for someone. Lena saw him too, and asked, "How does he come to be in such a state? Did he try to get away?"

I got up in a hurry. "Wait a moment. I'll come right back," I answered. And by running, I overtook him.

"Let's go home quickly," I said. "You look very suspicious. What are you looking for?"

"I'm trying to find Homer, to tell him that we didn't get away."

"Let's go home quickly," I repeated "I'll look for Homer and come back later."

He went home, and I returned to the cafe, being very careful on the way. Nothing suspicious. Lena was waiting for me. I explained to her in two words about their failure to get away. I didn't find Homer and went home in a hurry.

27 June 1944

Aleko Delmouzos[9] has long been one of our good friends.

[9] Alexander Delmouzos, great teacher, professor at the University of Thessalonika.

We admire and love him. Before the war he came regularly to our house. I remember many good discussions from those care-free days—endless discussions, about the language question and its development. Since the German invasion, Alecko has come to our house only seldom.

Suddenly this morning he was on the telephone.

"I want to see you as soon as possible," he said. "I'll wait for you at Zonar's cafe."

His voice was so altered that I answered without a second thought. "I'll come right away." And I left on the run.

I saw him sitting at a little table near the window. Pale, distracted, he was looking into the distance. I spoke first.

"Good morning, Mr. Delmouzos. What's the matter?"

"Sit down," he said, and took my hand. "They arrested Alkis yesterday." He was trembling all over and was so pale that I was frightened. I tried to be optimistic.

"Don't think the worst," I whispered. "He will be freed soon."

"Do me a favor," he answered. "When you leave your office, come for a moment and tell me what news you have. I'll wait for you from two o'clock on." I promised him and went away with a heavy heart.

Alkis Delmouzos[10] was in charge of the sabotage operations for APOLLO. I knew that after the arrest and execution of Nikos Adam, Alkis had taken his place. Now they have arrested him too. God alone can save him.

29 June 1944

Every morning, fearfully, I open the papers which come to the Archbishopric, and search through the names of the slain. I am on the alert for any news. And every noon I go past Zonar's.

"Alkis is alive," I tell him, and I enjoy seeing his bright eyes light up still more.

[10] Alkis Delmouzos, son of Alexander, with his brother, Panaghis, an engineer specializing in radio, worked with APOLLO from 1942.

30 June 1944

APOLLO (Advance Force 133) needs new personnel. Most of the old ones are burned out. They must be helped to get away. And now with the arrest of Alkis the danger is very great. Constantine Benakis[11] has taken on the responsibility for the reorganization and the administration of the service.

2 July 1944

My brother Angelos works at the secretariat of Advance Force 133.

This organization of Benakis takes care of all our obligations that arise from the occupation. Under his personal direction the various services operate with marvelous efficiency. Secretariat, code, postoffice, reception, radio, security, groups of the army, navy, and police, radio bulletins, daily newspaper *Eleutheria*, and sabotage. Each branch is perfectly organized, separate, and without contact with other sections.

In the requirement of absolute secrecy which this period imposes, this service is exemplary.

Constantine Benakis has good sense, courage, and a unique talent for organization. The virtues of a leader. But also the modesty that reveals his profound humanity.

3 July 1944

Stephen Doukas was asked to undertake the reorganization of the Sabotage Service of APOLLO. With Captain Verros and Lieutenant Toussas, he found some new warehouses, transferred the old materials, took delivery of the new ones, and organized the gangs of workers.

---

[11] Constantine Benakis, son of the donor of the Benaki Museum.

7 July 1944

In the new materials which Verros and Doukas received were some devices—called "turtles" and "mussels"[12] because of their shapes—which did not have an explosive system. They had to be filled with a special substance, easily formed, but with a strong odor of bitter almond.

Last night, while they were working in the warehouse on Beranger Street, they suddenly heard heavy steps on the pavement. They stopped their work and stood motionless. The steps came nearer, and soon reached the door. Then they clearly heard soldiers putting down their weapons, meanwhile speaking German.

"They've surrounded us," they thought. "We haven't even begun yet, but already we are betrayed."

Through the hole in the lowered shutter, our friends saw that the Germans were a squad of ten, fully armed. Ours had altogether two pistols and a small revolver. Before matching arms, they decided to wait. They remained motionless, and with difficulty held their breath, because the heavy odor of bitter almond was choking them and making them dizzy. They were also afraid that the odor would penetrate outside and the enemy would smell it.

For more than half an hour they were on the watch with hearts palpitating. Then they heard the weapons being lifted and the steps withdrawing.

"They had chosen that place to relax," Verros continued when he told me his story today. "What a scare they gave us!" And he smiled with relief.

12 July 1944

Yesterday at the Red Cross Hospital they arrested Lela Kara-

[12] The "turtle" was a sabotage-device in the shape of a turtle. It was made of metal and contained a large quantity of explosive, powerful magnets, and a special timer for setting it off. The "mussel" was a much smaller device whose shape suggested a mussel shell. It functioned in the same way as the "turtle."

yanni. A good many traitors are costing Greece dearly. One of them informed on her.

We all love and admire Lela. In our imagination she is almost a legend. She has a masculine soul, as Solomos says, a strong mind, and the instincts of the most perfect woman. With such virtues, her service is incalculable.

With her husband and children as collaborators, she devoted herself from the beginning to the first problem posed by the occupation: the escape of the Allies who remained behind in Greece at the time of the invasion. The Italians arrested her then, along with her husband, but released them because no evidence of guilt was found. Free once more, and wiser from experience, Lela extended her activity to all sectors of the resistance. In her organization she even had anti-Nazi Germans as informers.

15 July 1944

We are starting to prepare my husband's departure a second time. The day is set for the 19th of July. He has received the indispensable false identity card.

19 July 1944

This morning we have been gathering together the few things which he will take with him. He has been giving us his final instructions. Just as he is about to leave, he casts his eye over his papers to make sure he has his false identity card. But it is nowhere to be found. We turn the house upside-down, the same with the friend's house where he stayed last night. The false identity card has vanished.

Homer was waiting for him; there was no time to lose. He had to go with his own identity card.

I saw him off with a heavy heart. They had already arrested his cousin Admiral Tsatsos on the point of departure and had sentenced him to death. As for my husband's brother Themistocles, who had undertaken the Ministry of Justice in the Free Government, when they learned of his arrival in the Middle East, they invaded his house and ransacked it. Now a third Tsatsos is starting out with his real name. If they take him, he will not escape.[13]

Black thoughts take possession of me. What saves me is my faith in God.

22 July 1944

From Turkey the news reached us that they arrived safe and sound, what a relief! These past three days were unbearable.

23 July 1944

I have to remove from my house everything of value. Every day I expect the invasion of the Germans.

3 August 1944

Moving all day. My house seems empty, impersonal. Whatever was beautiful, whatever I loved is gone. The things around me are remote, indifferent, and the habits of so many years, even these have vanished.

[13] When Costakis returned, he explained to me how the disappearance of his false identity card had been his salvation. On the way, the Germans stopped the bus, made a search, and found a German can of meat in his knapsack. They were angry, accused him of having robbed the German army, and told him to follow them. They took him out of the bus alone. They asked for his identity card and Costakis gave them the only one he had, the true one. Immediately their attitude changed. They gave him a military salute and asked his pardon, addressing him as "Herr Professor." They had read on his card that he was a professor of the University and were instantly persuaded that he had not robbed the German army. They released him to go on with the others.

The day is over. Its pain and its labor. I am no longer in a hurry. Just some more waiting.

15 August 1944

In his isolation, the Archbishop has transformed one room of his house into a chapel. There he regularly celebrates the Divine Liturgy, all alone. And today there took place the most mystical liturgy of Panayia, the Virgin. We were given permission to attend. The atmosphere of devotion was deep.

No date

I had not seen Apostolos for a good many days. Yesterday he came by in the evening. He seemed uneasy.

"Did you know?" he said. "The Germans have arrested Elias."[14]

I was desolate.

"We must save him somehow," I answered. "They say that the Gestapo now accepts money."

"I'm doing all I can," he continued, "but I must find the key. If I succeed, can you hide him in your house?"

"Of course," I said.

No date

Five or six days have passed and Apostolos has not reappeared. I have no way of communicating with him. He has changed his address again, and his telephone does not answer.

No date

Apostolos came with Elias. What a joy for both me and my children! Apostolos told us all about his transactions with the

[14] Elias Athanassiadis, officer in the 5/42 Regiment.

114

Nazi officer. In the beginning, half the money, and when he delivered Elias, the remaining sovereigns.

No date

Elias has stayed with us. He was ill, but soon he became well again. Despina and Dora have undertaken to entertain him. They play chess with him.

At first we were all careful, even about our shadows. But then, as the days pass, we become more daring. Elias begins to go out in the evening, and he goes back and forth between the two floors of the house. We have introduced him to Eudoxia as a friend from the country.

Happily all goes well.

28 August 1944

The S.D. has left Greece. The country is purged of a good many criminals.

After the departure of the S.D., no German service has dared to intervene in the detention of the Archbishop. Very early this morning we learned that he would come down to his office: Philothei Street was full of people. He was late, and every one was impatient to see him. When at last they saw him, they could not contain their emotion.

"Don't ever leave us again!" they shouted, and they wept and threw flowers.

The people have found themselves again.

5 September 1944

From day before yesterday, hours of frightful anguish. Great losses to the Fifth Sabotage Team of APOLLO. Andreas Chara-lambopoulos was assigned to blow up the destroyer *Turbine*.

He had started for the Naval Base, but he was too daring. He was not enough on his guard about the German sentry. They arrested him at the very moment when he was putting the bomb in place.

Now the Germans want to learn everything and to arrest everyone. Charalambopoulos does not confess, and he begins his martyrdom which will last till death. They cut his legs, they put out his eyes, they break his bones, and fortunately he dies of hemorrhage.

This was the condition in which they found his body, thrown out at the end of Liossion Street. During his terrible sufferings, one name escaped him, that of Basil Giannakopoulos.

They rush to his sister's house. They beat her and ask her where her brother is. She does not answer. Then they wake up her children, lay them out on the floor, and put pistols to their temples. Terrorized, the woman gives the address where her brother is hidden.

Another martyrdom for Basil: they hung him by his arm so that for a long time his hand was useless.

At his sister's house they found a note containing the name of Charalambidis who works at the Commandant's office. They rushed to arrest him. They threatened him. And he, knowing that Major Doukas was not at home, implicated him.

The Nazis broke down the door of Doukas' house, and went in with their automatics drawn. There they found his wife with her little boy and her parents. Fortunately for them, they all speak German.

General Digenis, Helen Doukas' father, showed some false papers and persuaded the Germans that his daughter had been separated from her husband for a long time and that he had indeed abandoned her. So they went away, without bothering anybody and without looting the house as they were accustomed to do when they made arrests.

Charalambidis knew that the warehouse of Beranger Street no longer contained sabotage materials. He gave them that address. They got there at six in the morning. They broke the iron shutters and burst in, thinking they would find the material. But the storeroom was empty. Nothing but some cans of soup in a corner.

6 September 1944

This morning Doukas arrived at our house, unshaven, eyes red from lack of sleep. Maria was here too.

"I can't go home," said Stephen. "The Germans have been there. I think that I left a paper in a cupboard, and I must get hold of it. They may come back."

"I'll go," said Maria immediately.

"But it's I who will go. It's my job," I answered.

Stephen then made the decision: "Better that Maria should go. You know too much."

So Maria went. She reached Doukas' house. Beautiful and blonde, she went nonchalantly upstairs, as if it were of no importance, opened the cupboard, found nothing there, and came back. In the street she made sure that she was not being followed.

Her return brought us great relief.

9 September 1944

Mute and rebellious, these days we follow the doings of this beast, this hangman called Bache, who every day invents new torture to try to make Lela Karayanni speak. Little by little her body is dying, but her secret remains secret.

From what faith does her great soul derive this strength of the early Christians? She offers husband, children, her own life, all these sacrifices, human and superhuman, that Greece may be free.

They executed her yesterday at Haidari, along with seventy other brave souls.

At the final moment, covered with wounds, she asked to lead

the dance—like the heroines of the Greek Revolution—so as to give courage to the others about to die.

10 September 1944

In front of my office window is a gray wall, all of a piece, like a stage curtain, a barrier. Nothing blue. Nothing green. Only at one point pops up a chimney, and in this chimney, a redthroat has built her nest. She goes and comes again, twittering and bringing food to her little ones.

God's little bird, only this, brings back to us some far-off sense of life.

17 September 1944

When this woman came into the room, I looked up, because I sensed a change in the atmosphere. She wore a black fur coat, and she stood there, tall, straight, with her snow-white hair. Her eyes, fixed on some invisible point, like the eyes of the blind, seemed to see nothing. Her words came out with difficulty: "Before I die, I must speak to someone," she whispered to me. She sat down near me and began this incredible account.

"The enemy entered Salonica. We lived there together, my son Demetri and I. One day they knocked at our door, and a German officer established himself in our house. My son and I took refuge in the remaining room. Plunged in hate and grief as we were, under the great affliction of slavery, we couldn't stand even to look at his face.

"But time passed. The days, the weeks, the year. The stranger was polite, careful, educated, and, above all, young, very young, like my son. Unconsciously, we began to distinguish him from the rest of the Germans. We invited him to eat with us. He talked to us about his mother, about his deep homesickness. We invited him again and again. And finally, without our thinking much about it, every evening his plate was there on our table.

"Demetri and Peter became inseparable companions. They loved the same poetry, the same music, they read the same books. I can still hear the Bach Cantatas they played together on the gramophone. As an exercise, Peter tried, with the help of my son, to translate Thucydides into German. Endless discussions on philosophical subjects filled their evening hours. And this relationship, during three whole years, turned into brotherly affection. A deep, common European culture had united them, far, very far away from the catastrophe and the crime. . . . Far from the crime. . . . Not so far. . . .

"A month before, as the Russians were advancing toward the heart of Germany, Peter had become gloomy. He had no news of his mother. His concern gave him not a moment's peace."

The woman took a deep breath. For the first time she looked straight at me, her blue eyes turned to stone, stupefied, while they searched for something beyond life.

"It was a Wednesday afternoon," she went on—"at four o'clock. We had had coffee, the young men chatting of this and that, absorbed, as they were, in other thoughts. Peter sighed again. Then Demetri, with the compassion of friendship, and like a Greek—who finds political solutions easy—leaned over and said to him, 'Why do you hang on to this Hitler? Don't you see that everything in your country is collapsing? Make a revolution and capitulate as quickly as possible.'

"He had scarcely finished his sentence when the whole world seemed to crumble around us. The Nazi got up quickly, took his cap, gave a military salute, and disappeared. We looked at each other in astonishment, unable to comprehend the disaster that awaited us. Some hours later Demetri was arrested. I never saw him again. They told me where he was buried. Nor did I see Peter again."

In her eyes one saw the horror of the void—her hands trembled.

"I don't understand," she said, "I had been like a mother to him, when he was sick, when he was unhappy. . . ."

Mechanically she opened her handbag and gave me the last piece of paper she had found in Demetri's desk, a paper written in thin letters. There seemed to be verses, erased and rewritten, of which only the last line was clear: "Now I can no longer give you birth. . . ."

"It is a translation of the *Pieta* of Rilke," I whispered in awe, as I held her hand.

. . . .

And they say that beauty liberates. . . .

19 September 1944

I go about among people as in a thick forest full of thorns. They scratch me and they hurt me. One with his misfortune and unhappiness, another with his lies, another with his wickedness. After a few steps, I feel my nerves shattered, my skin inflamed and bleeding.

But a haunting song, very low, begins to be heard inside me. I cannot find the words to fit it, but it seems to give me some very small understanding of the measureless wisdom and beauty of God. Something is helping me to find the synthesis, and more than that, the poetry of human tragedy. Perhaps it is a momentary miracle, some help in the midst of desperation.

20 September 1944

Night. The Furies, like snakes, lie charmed and motionless at my feet, shapes of slavery. And the only honest thing—the miracle of the night. I feel such faith within me, such love, in the primitive meaning of that word, something of that love which God felt on the day of Creation. If the earth died, I would aid in its resurrection—it is enough that the stars are there, speaking to me as they speak to me tonight.

22 September 1944

Helen Nika is very free with us. Ever since 1941 when the Germans killed her husband, she comes regularly from Eleusis directly to us for whatever she needs. This morning she seemed very worried. "Madame," she said to me, "sit down and write a letter for me to Captain Nikitas,[15] asking him to give up my house. Otherwise something dreadful will happen. I'm in the street with my child. Don't you understand?"

"What are you saying, Helen my girl? Have you lost your senses?" I answered her. "I've never seen Captain Nikitas. I don't know him. So how could I write him a letter? If I do, I'm likely to do you more harm than good. And then, the Germans are still here—what if they arrest you?"

But Helen insisted, and wept, and people crowded the office, and she wept still more. So I sat down and wrote:

Captain Nikitas, relinquish the house belonging to Helen Nika, and protect her, because the Germans killed her husband and she has an orphan child to bring up.

Ioanna Tsatsos.

Helen took the letter and hurried off.[16]

24 September 1944

Rumors and news. Landing in Europe. Revolts. Paris is free. A hope of triumph begins timidly to rise, but again the taste of ashes, the frozen desolation of partings.

Marjorie Dimopoulos' mother came to our office. So very sad. Her daughter was executed on the 8th of September. Some one had dropped a word about the landing.

"If she had escaped death for one month, she would never have died," she said to me softly, and her lips puckered in bitterness.

28 September 1944

At last the first representatives of the Greek government have arrived. The Chief of Police telephoned me to go to the Police

[15] Communist leader.
[16] Ten days later she returned in triumph. Captain Nikitas had left the house.

121

Station to meet Mistos Tsatsos. That's where they are putting him up. I rushed there immediately, overwhelmed with emotion. I listened to him, absorbing every word. News of Costakis, which I awaited for so long, news of George Seferis, political news, news of the war. Everything was encouraging. Life seems to begin again.

1 October 1944

We feel that every hour is bringing us nearer to the end. Our hope takes on gigantic dimensions. We struggle with Fate to win the great day of peace for Greece.

The Archbishop has taken over an Italian warehouse, full of fine capes, and every day we distribute them to the naked people who receive them with a double joy—as clothing and as booty.

3 October 1944

The Archbishopric was full of refugees. On every stair, women with babies. The children cried, and so did their mothers. The men silent, withdrawn. Old women raved in the corners.

"What's going on?" I asked the secretary.

"A terrible thing at Ai-Yannis," he answered.

"What happened?" I asked a man sitting on the stairs.

"Communists attacked a German auto and killed two Germans," he explained. "From that moment the Gestapo has been killing people at random and devastating their houses. They are all fleeing in terror, seeking protection anywhere."

With these last words, the weeping and sobbing increased.

What to do? There must have been about seventy people. We had very little money. The Archbishop was away at the time.

I got the Chief of Police on the telephone. "Mr. Evert," I begged, "Can you requisition a hotel for a few days for the refugees from Ai-Yannis? They can't go home. Their lives are in danger."

"I'll do it," he answered. "I'll send you two policemen to guide them."

The Chief of Police has one remarkable quality. He decides and acts with great speed. After about an hour, the people from Ai-Yannis had been conducted to a small hotel near Omonia Square.

We gave each one enough money for three or four days.

4 October 1944

The shouting of the Communists in Kydathineon Street— "Long live Zevgos!"—grows gradually less. I sit for a while and watch the night come on. Because always the nights help me find again the soul that I have lost. Tonight again I haven't the strength to escape it. All things are silent before its silence. What endures is the black sombre line of the cypress at the Church of the Savior, pointing unfailingly to God.

7 October 1944

The Germans will go, indeed they are already going, but it is inconceivable. Yesterday again they shot twenty-five persons.

Why do people confide so many things in me? Perhaps because I am marked as one whose lips are sealed with silence. Silence which is both a law and a necessity. I am a deep well into which I throw quickly all the secrets, the dreams, the grievances and the claims, the fears and the homesickness—and I cover it all over with a stone cover. Its depths are shaken, and then I feel I am lost. How weak I am now!

10 October 1944

The whole world in the streets—how strange! What do they expect to hear? What do they expect to see? The Germans are still here.

12 October 1944

The long blood-stained march has brought us to the summit.

God is there, and now He will bless the tears of our anguish and bitterness.

I open the windows wide. Light, the sun, the blue sky. Together with my children I watch with devout concentration a point opposite us on the Acropolis. For us it is the center of the world.

And we see the German flag slowly, slowly descend, see it disappear as if the Sacred Rock had swallowed it. And there begins to rise in its place the beloved color of our sky. My brimming eyes can no longer see. But when I have managed quickly to dry my tears, the Blue and the White waves proudly in the breeze.

Greece is once more our own, our very own.

We have won her with our blood, our toil, with daily privation, but above all we have won her in the dark grief of all our years of slavery.

Greece is once more our own.

This is justice. This is how things are meant to be.

I scarcely know what to do. I seize the Allied flags which they have given me and go out into the streets. I hurry to the Archbishopric. I want to see Frank Macaskey. They telephone to me that he has arrived.

The people are mad with joy. They kiss each other. They weep. They wait for the English to come.

In Constitution Square I meet a German company going forward to lay a wreath on the tomb of the Unknown Soldier. The officer takes note of the flags I am carrying and glares at me. But I hurry on to the Archbishopric.

Macaskey has arrived there with a little suitcase in his hand. The Archbishop receives him with emotion.

"If you are really a British officer," he says to him, teasing, "where is your uniform?"

"Here," answers Frank, pointing to his suitcase.

"Put it on," orders the Archbishop.

Macaskey goes into the next room and returns shortly—an English officer.

And then the two of them get into an open automobile and go out among the crowds.

The people cheer them enthusiastically. "The Englishman!" they shout, and lift the automobile with their hands. They try to touch Macaskey, and he smiles back at them with affection. With the boundless affection he has for Greece.

When the Archbishop and Macaskey go out on the balcony of Damaskinos' house to greet the crowds, it is as if the lungs of the whole world would burst. So great the joy in the voice of the people.

13 October 1944

"The place whereon thou standest is holy ground." (Exodus 3:5). A curse on whoever stains it, be he foreigner or traitor, Nemesis is inexorable.

God's justice spreads out as on the day of the Last Judgment, and all of us together, living and dead, are the instruments of His justice.

The whole of this day, the tears and the anguish of the imprisoned and the dead, and of the other sorrowing Greeks, are transmuted into work and a wild joy.

The whole of this day, the Greeks like lovers are united with their earth. No grief can enter in. The endless trial gives to this moment its divine meaning. Our souls are full of prayer and thanksgiving.

All of us gather in the Cathedral. It is the first *Te Deum* for Archbishop Damaskinos.

Standing erect, the Archbishop chants the praises which he himself has composed.

> *Ye shades of the heroic dead,*
> *Ye hosts of the living,*
> *Ye myriads of victims,*

Ye rows of graves,
Ye swarms of mourners,
With tears of rejoicing,
Bless ye the Lord!

Suddenly the whole church vibrates with the age-old hymn of Orthodoxy. Archbishop, priests, choir, and congregation sing together:

To Her, the Virgin,
Invincible Leader in battle,
To Her the trophies of victory - - - -

Rejoicing — Redemption.

I fall on my knees. And with the rest, I try to add my voice, broken with tears, in praise of Panayia, the All-Holy Virgin.

Index

Adam, Nikos, 77–78
Aghia Barbara (suburb of Athens), 5
Ai-Yannis, refugees from, 122–123
Ajax, 97
Akylas, Michalis, 24; poem by, quoted, 25–27
Alevizakis, Elias, 44
Alevizatos, Constantine, 53n
Alexi (liaison officer), 77
Amphissa: liberation of, 79–80; Germans attempt to retake, 94–95
Andronikos (radio operator), 62
Androutsos, quoted, 64
Antigone (girl from Plaka), 9
Anti-Paros affair, 45–47
APOLLO (secret organization: Advance Force 133), 77–78, 109, 110; Fifth Sabotage Team of, 115–116; attempted sabotage of destroyer Turbine, 115–116
Argyrocastro, Albania, ix
Argyropoulou, Fotini, 15
"Ark," Allied Operation, 96
Arvanitopoulous. See Kypriadis
Asyrmato (suburb of Athens), 12
Athanasiadis, Thanasis, 95–96
Athanassiadis, Elias, 114–115
Atkinson, John, 45–46
Averof, George, 3
Averoff Prison, 30–31, 46, 47

Bach, Johann Sebastian, 119
Barkas family, 24–25
Benakis, Constantine, 110
Boukas (radio-telegrapher), 34
Bouras, Costas, 62–64

Byron Street, office of relief organization, 13–14, 17

Calvos, To the Sacred Legion, quoted, 39
Charalambopoulos, Andreas, 115–117
Chartsa, Kyrá, 58–60
Commando Piazza, 59, 60, 73
Communist party, xi, 21, 54, 66, 96, 121, 122, 123. See also ELAS
Conte de Savoia, sinking of, 77

Damaskinos, Archbishop: mentioned, xi; begins relief work for families of executed Greeks, 6, 21; advises author about husband's security, 10; seeks pardon for Ghini brothers, 23; meets with Tsigantes, 41; gets permission to open common grave, 41–42; attempts to save Constantine Perrikos, 43; establishes Pan-Hellenic Fund, 45; plans to lead march through Athens, 51–52; attack of angina, 51; directs application of Pan-Hellenic Fund, 52–53, 55; receives Italian protest against relief activities, 54; attempts to save Greek Jews, 56; comforts bereaved families, 61–62; intercedes with Italians in behalf of Christos Karvounis, 65; finds funds to aid Psarros' officers, 68; and reprisal of Nazis for burning of Kallithea station, 71–73; and surrender of Italians, 73–74; and

Damaskinos, Archbishop (*Cont.*)
APOLLO, 78; and identifying of
victims at Kaissariani, 99–101;
arrest and detention of, 104–106,
114; release of, 115; distributes
Italian clothing to Greeks, 122;
at end of occupation, 124–126
Danielidis (radio operator), 61, 62
Dedoussis, Captain, 80
Deimezis, Alexander, 87–89
Delmouzos, Alexander, 108n, 108–
109
Delmouzos, Alkis, 109
Dimopoulos, Marjorie, 121
Distomo (village in Boeotia), ravaged by Nazis, 106–107
Doukas, Captain Stephen: liaison
agent for Tsigantes, 33; brings
news of Tsigantes' death, 42; and
counterespionage, 43; as leader
in resistance movement, 67–68;
mentioned, 82n, 85; en route with
Athanasiadis, 95–96; as representative of Psarros, 96; eludes ELAS
guerrillas, 98; reorganizes Sabotage Service of APOLLO, 110–
111; home of entered by Nazis,
116–117
Doussi, Katina: hides British soldier, 3; arrested by Italians, 14–
15; contact with Angelos Seferiades in prison, 30–31

EAM-ELAS (Communist-led resistance group). *See* ELAS
EDES (resistance group), xi
EKKA (resistance group headed by
Colonel Psarros), xi, 21n, 29, 50,
62, 82n, 83, 98
ELAS (EAM-ELAS, resistance movement): led by Communists, xi, 96;
author avoids joining, 21; 5/42
Evzones attacked by, 65–66; Kartalis confronts leaders of, 67;
comments of Psarros on, 82; in
battle against Germans, 86, 107;
avoid unification of resistance efforts, 96; Psarros killed by guerrillas of, 97–98
Eleutheria (daily newspaper), 110
ESPO (traitorous organization), 35–
36

Eudoxia (maid in Tsatsos household), 9, 89, 101
Evert (Chief of Police), 122–123
Evzones, 5/42 regiment, commanded
by Colonel Psarros: recognized
as ready for battle, 50; attacked
by ELAS, 65–66; good news from,
67; joining of by Rural Police, 73;
reconstituted, 79–80; occupy Amphissa, 94n; turn back Germans
at Roumeli, 95; and Allied Operation "Ark," 96; 150 men of killed
by ELAS guerrillas, 97; aid to survivors of ELAS massacre, 98
Exodus (Old Testament), quoted,
125

Fefé, Mrs. (woman of Kalavrita),
86–87
Fund for Those Who Are Detained,
55. *See also* Pan-Hellenic Fund

Galiotis, Sergeant (resistance sol-
dier), 95
George II, King of the Hellenes, x
German News for Greece (news-
paper), 50
Getsali, Kyrá, 32–33
Ghini family, 23
Giannakopoulos, Basil, 116
Gide, André, *The Prodigal Son*, 5
Goutis, André, 63n

Haidari, prisoners held at, 87–88,
117
Heraclitus, quoted, 73
Hitler, Adolf, ix
"Homer" (pseudonym of Dionysios
Verros), 107

Jeff, Captain (English officer), 57
Jews, baptism of, 56
John (New Testament), quoted, 103

Kaimaras, Captain (resistance of-
ficer), 94
Kairis (Greek patriot), 79
Kaissariani, execution of hostages
at, 99–104
Kalabouras, Evanthia, 27
Kalavrita, burning of, 86–87

Kallithea (suburb of Athens), burning of station at, 71–73
Kanaris, Elias, 47–49
Kanellopoulos, Panayiotis, 24
Kapoussidis, Costas, 77
Kapsalopoulos, Apostolos: and organization of EKKA, 29; as bringer of news of resistance movement, 50, 65, 67, 80, 94; and financial aid to officers of resistance, 68; mentioned, 70, 83; secures release of Athanassiadis by Germans, 114–115
Karamanlis, Costas, 34–35
Karayanni, Lela: seized by Italians, 4; arrested by Germans, 111–112; execution of, 117–118
Kartalis, George: identified, 21–22; and organization of EKKA, 29; makes contact with A. Seferiades at Lamia, 32; as contact with Psarros, 50; brings news of ELAS attack on regiment of Psarros, 65–66; confronts ELAS leaders, 67; brings news from resistance and from Seferis in Egypt, 80–83; leaves to rejoin regiment, 85–86; en route with Athanasiadis, 95–96; appointed representative of Psarros, 96; brings news of Psarros' death, 97; leaves for Middle East, 99
Karvounis, Dr. Christos: identified, 11n; on the war and necessity for resistance, 11–12; arrested by Italians, 64–65; freed, 76; shot by Nazis, 84–85
Katsimbalis, George, 50
Kokorelis (brother of resistance officer), 98
Koritsa, Albania, ix
Kydathineon Street, Tsatsos home in, 3n, 58
Kypriadis (pseudonym of Arvanitopoulos, radio-telegraph operator), 46–47
Kyriakou, Rena, 55

Laggouranis, Lieutenant Colonel, 79
Lamia, 31–33, 35
Levesque, Robert, 5
Levidis, Admiral Alekos, 4n

Lidoriki, abandoned by Germans, 80
"Life for the Child" movement, 16 and 16n, 22
Luke (New Testament), quoted, 102

Macaskey, Frank, 74n, 74–76, 124–125
Manilla, sinking of, 77
Mastoris, Yannis, 34
Metaxas, John, Greek Premier, 7
Middle East Command, x–xi, 11, 50, 62, 67
Miller, Henry, The Colossus of Maroussi, 50n
Monodendri (Sparta), 117 men shot by Nazis at, 84–85
Mussolini, Benito, ix
Myrophyllo (village), 96
Mytilinaios (resistance soldier), 36

Neubacher (officer of German Occupation), 72, 105
New Smyrna (suburb of Athens), 62
Nika, Helen, 120–121
Nikitas, Captain (Communist leader), 121

Olga Boulevard, battle on, 81
Olympia Theatre, benefit for Fund at, 55–56
Omonia, battle at, 86

Palamas, Costis, 49–50
Panayia (the Virgin Mary), 69, 102, 114, 126
Panayiotis, Charidis, 15
Pan-Hellenic Fund: established by Archbishop Damaskinos, 45; operation of, 52–54; benefit concert for, 55–56; Italian attempt to sink, 60
Pankrati (section of Athens), 80
Papakyriazis, Colonel, 31, 35
Papas, Roxane, wife of Angelos Seferiades, 28 and 28n, 29
Parnassos Hall, 36
PEAN (Panhellenic Union of Young Fighters), 36, 43n
Perrikos, Constantine: leader of PEAN, 35–37, 35n; execution of, 43–44
Pertouli (village in Thessaly), 67

Pezmazoglou, John, 71n
Phaneromeni, monastery at Salamis, 10
Philothei Street, Archbishop's offices in, 74, 115
Plaka (Section of Athens), 3n, 9, 14, 16, 22
Plato, *Phaedo*, quoted, 61
Poubourra, Alexandra, 15
Psarros, Colonel Demetrius: leader of EKKA (resistance group), xi; regiment of recognized as battle-ready, 50; aid for regiment of, 57; resisting attacks of ELAS, 65–66; leaves for resistance activities in Pertouli, 67; aid to officers of, 68–71; and liberation of Roumeli, 79–80; news of from Kartalis, 82; occupation of Amphissa by, 94n; resists Germans at Roumeli, 94–95; and Allied Operation "Ark," 96; death of, 97, 98–99; mentioned, 21 and 21n, 55, 62, 73, 75
Psychiko (section of Athens), 51, 68, 74, 75, 76, 105, 106

Red Cross, 13, 24, 45, 53, 53n, 56, 84, 100, 111
Resistance movement summarized, ix–xi. *See also* EKKA; ELAS; Psarros; Damaskinos, Archbishop; Evzones, 5/42 regiment
Richardson, John, 15
Rilke, Rainer Maria, 120
Rommel, Erwin, German field marshal, 22, 35
Roumeli (popular name for a region of Greece), liberation of, 79–80
Roussos (radio operator), 62

Samartzi's cafe, 63, 80–81
Santa Fe, attempted sinking of, 77
Seferiades, Angelos (brother of author): illness of, 28–29, 30–34, 35; confined in Averoff Prison, 30–31; transferred to Lamia, 31; contact made with, 32; returns home, 33–34; at secretariat of APOLLO, 110
Seferis, George (brother of author): poems translated by Levesque, 5n;

in Egypt, 66; identified, 66n; news of, from Egypt, 82, 122
S. D. [Sicherheitsdienst], 105, 106, 115
Sikelianos, Angelos (Greek poet), 5n, 49
Socrates, 47, 61
Solomos, Dionysios, *Ode to Liberty*, quoted, 50
Sparta, 117 men executed by Nazis at, 84
Speidel, German general, 71, 72, 76
Supreme National Council, organization of, 33

Theophilou, arrested, 77–78
Theotokas, George, 53n, 70
Theotokas, Lilika, 53
To My Death (Poem), quoted, 104
Toussas, Lieutenant, 110
Tsatsos, Constantine (Costakis; husband of author): first sought by police, 6–8; arrest and detention in 1939, 7n; dismissed from University, 8; and organization of EKKA, 29; and organization of Supreme National Council, 33–34, 41; seeks aid for Psarros' officers, 68; attempt to leave Athens, 108; second attempt to leave Athens, 112–113; reaches Turkey, 113
Tsatsos, Despina (daughter of author), 7, 16, 59, 93, 101, 115
Tsatsos, Dora (daughter of author), 7, 16, 22, 85, 89, 93, 101, 115
Tsatsos, Themistocles (Mistos; brother of Constantine Tsatsos), 75–76, 113, 122
Tsatsos, Admiral (cousin of Constantine Tsatsos), 112
Tsigantes, John (Yannis): identified, 29n; plans for resistance, 29–30; and organization of Supreme National Council, 33–34; secret meeting with Constantine Tsatsos, 41; death of, 42–43; mentioned, 62
Turbine (destroyer), attempted sabotage of, 115–117
Tzavellas (lawyer), 45–47
Tzivanopoulos brothers, 85

Vassaras (village on Mount Parnis), 11 and 11n

130

Verros, Dionysios ("Homer"), 107n; helps reorganize Sabotage Service of APOLLO, 110–111

Vlachos, Major, 82

Yannatos, Costas, 41
Yannatos, Demetrius, 41
Yatrakis, letter of wife of, 52n–53n

Zannas, Aleko: arrested by Italians, 24; trial of, 45; imprisonment, 47
Zarifi, Lena, 83–85, 93–94
Zervas (resistance leader of EDES): identified, 21n; mentioned, xi, 21, 55, 73
Zonar's cafe, 109